The Type Astronaut's Guide to Shapeless

April 2017

Published by Underscore Consulting LLP, Brighton, UK.

Contents

Foreword

Back at the beginning of 2011, when I first started doing the experiments in generic programming that would eventually turn into shapeless, I had no idea that five years later it would have evolved into such a widely used library. I am profoundly grateful to the people who have trusted me and added shapeless as a dependency to their own projects: the vote of confidence that this represents is a huge motivator for any open source project. I am also hugely grateful to the many people who have contributed to shapeless over the years: eighty one at the time of writing. Without their help shapeless would be a far less interesting and useful library.

These positives notwithstanding, shapeless has suffered from one of the common failings of open source projects: a lack of comprehensive, accurate and accessible documentation. The responsibility for this lies squarely at my door: despite acknowledging the lack I have never been able to find the time to do anything about it. To some extent shapeless has been saved from this by Travis Brown's heroic Stack Overflow performance and also by the many people who have given talks about and run workshops on shapeless (in particular I'd like to highlight Sam Halliday's "Shapeless for Mortals" workshop).

But Dave Gurnell has changed all that: we now have this wonderful book length treatment of shapeless's most important application: type class derivation via generic programming. In doing this he has pulled together fragments of folklore and documentation, has picked my brain, and turned the impenetrable tangle into something which is clear, concise and very practical. With any luck he will be able to make good on my regular claims that at its core shapeless is a very simple library embodying a set of very simple concepts.

Thanks Dave, you've done us all a great service.

Miles Sabin
Creator of shapeless

Chapter 1

Introduction

This book is a guide to using shapeless[1], a library for *generic programming* in Scala. Shapeless is a large library, so rather than cover everything it has to offer we will concentrate on a few compelling use cases and use them to build a picture of the tools and patterns available.

Before we start, let's talk about what generic programming is and why shapeless is so exciting to Scala developers.

1.1   What is generic programming?

Types are helpful because they are specific: they show us how different pieces of code fit together, help us prevent bugs, and guide us toward solutions when we code.

Sometimes, however, types are *too* specific. There are situations where we want to exploit similarities between types to avoid repetition. For example, consider the following definitions:

---

[1]https://github.com/milessabin/shapeless

3

```
case class Employee(name: String, number: Int, manager: Boolean)

case class IceCream(name: String, numCherries: Int, inCone: Boolean)
```

These two case classes represent different kinds of data but they have clear similarities: they both contain three fields of the same types. Suppose we want to implement a generic operation such as serializing to a CSV file. Despite the similarity between the two types, we have to write two separate serialization methods:

```
def employeeCsv(e: Employee): List[String] =
  List(e.name, e.number.toString, e.manager.toString)

def iceCreamCsv(c: IceCream): List[String] =
  List(c.name, c.numCherries.toString, c.inCone.toString)
```

Generic programming is about overcoming differences like these. Shapeless makes it convenient to convert specific types into generic ones that we can manipulate with common code.

For example, we can use the code below to convert employees and ice creams to values of the same type. Don't worry if you don't follow this example yet— we'll get to grips with the various concepts later on:

```
import shapeless._

val genericEmployee = Generic[Employee].to(Employee("Dave", 123, false))
// genericEmployee: String :: Int :: Boolean :: shapeless.HNil = Dave ::
//     123 :: false :: HNil

val genericIceCream = Generic[IceCream].to(IceCream("Sundae", 1, false))
// genericIceCream: String :: Int :: Boolean :: shapeless.HNil = Sundae
//     :: 1 :: false :: HNil
```

Both values are now of the same type. They are both heterogeneous lists (HLists for short) containing a String, an Int, and a Boolean. We'll look at HLists and the important role they play soon. For now the point is that we can serialize each value with the same function:

```
def genericCsv(gen: String :: Int :: Boolean :: HNil): List[String] =
  List(gen(0), gen(1).toString, gen(2).toString)

genericCsv(genericEmployee)
// res2: List[String] = List(Dave, 123, false)

genericCsv(genericIceCream)
// res3: List[String] = List(Sundae, 1, false)
```

This example is basic but it hints at the essence of generic programming. We reformulate problems so we can solve them using generic building blocks, and write small kernels of code that work with a wide variety of types. Generic programming with shapeless allows us to eliminate huge amounts of boilerplate, making Scala applications easier to read, write, and maintain.

Does that sound compelling? Thought so. Let's jump in!

1.2   About this book

This book is divided into two parts.

In Part I we introduce *type class derivation*, which allows us to create type class instances for any algebraic data type using only a handful of generic rules. Part I consists of four chapters:

- In Chapter 2 we introduce *generic representations*. We also introduce shapeless' Generic type class, which can produce a generic encoding for any case class or sealed trait.

- In Chapter 3 we use Generic to derive instances of a custom type class. We create an example type class to encode Scala data as Comma Separated Values (CSV), but the techniques we cover can be extended to many situations. We also introduce shapeless' Lazy type, which lets us handle recursive data like lists and trees.

- In Chapter 4 we introduce the theory and programming patterns we need to generalise the techniques from earlier chapters. Specifically we look at dependent types, dependently typed functions, and type level programming. This allows us to access more advanced applications of shapeless.

- In Chapter 5 we introduce `LabelledGeneric`, a variant of `Generic` that exposes field and type names as part of its generic representations. We also introduce additional theory: literal types, singleton types, phantom types, and type tagging. We demonstrate `LabelledGeneric` by creating a JSON encoder that preserves field and type names in its output.

In Part II we introduce the "ops type classes" provided in the `shapeless.ops` package. Ops type classes form an extensive library of tools for manipulating generic representations. Rather than discuss every op in detail, we provide a theoretical primer in three chapters:

- In Chapter 6 we discuss the general layout of the ops type classes and provide an example that strings several simple ops together to form a powerful "case class migration" tool.

- In Chapter 7 we introduce *polymorphic functions*, also known as `Poly`s, and show how they are used in ops type classes for mapping, flat mapping, and folding over generic representations.

- Finally, in Chapter 8 we introduce the `Nat` type that shapeless uses to represent natural numbers at the type level. We introduce several related ops type classes, and use `Nat` to develop our own version of Scalacheck's `Arbitrary`.

1.3   Source code and examples

This book is open source. You can find the Markdown source on Github[2]. The book receives constant updates from the community so be sure to check the Github repo for the most up-to-date version.

---

[2]https://github.com/underscoreio/shapeless-guide

We also maintain a copy of the book on the Underscore web site[3]. If you grab a copy of the book from there we will notify you whenever we release an update.

There are complete implementations of the major examples in an accompanying repo[4]. See the README for installation details. We assume shapeless 2.3.2 and either Typelevel Scala 2.11.8+ or Lightbend Scala 2.11.9+ / 2.12.1+.

Most of the examples in this book are compiled and executed using version 2.12.1 of the Typelevel Scala compiler. Among other niceties this version of Scala introduces *infix type printing*, which cleans up the console output on the REPL:

```
val repr = "Hello" :: 123 :: true :: HNil
// repr: String :: Int :: Boolean :: shapeless.HNil = Hello :: 123 ::
     true :: HNil
```

If you are using an older version of Scala you might end up with prefix type printing like this:

```
val repr = "Hello" :: 123 :: true :: HNil
// repr: shapeless.::[String,shapeless.::[Int,shapeless.::[Boolean,
     shapeless.HNil]]] = "Hello" :: 123 :: true :: HNil
```

Don't panic! Aside from the printed form of the result (infix versus prefix syntax), these types are the same. If you find the prefix types difficult to read, we recommend upgrading to a newer version of Scala. Simply add the following to your build.sbt, substituting in contemporary version numbers as appropriate:

```
scalaOrganization := "org.typelevel"
scalaVersion      := "2.12.1"
```

The scalaOrganization setting is only supported in SBT 0.13.13 or later. You can specify an SBT version by writing the following in project/build.properties (create the file if it isn't there in your project):

---

[3]https://underscore.io/books/shapeless-guide
[4]https://github.com/underscoreio/shapeless-guide-code

```
sbt.version=0.13.13
```

1.4   Acknowledgements

Thanks to Miles Sabin, Richard Dallaway, Noel Welsh, Travis Brown, and our fellow space-farers on Github[5] for their invaluable contributions to this guide.

Special thanks to Sam Halliday for this excellent workshop Shapeless for Mortals[6], which provided the initial inspiration and skeleton.

Finally, thanks to Rob Norris and his fellow contributors for the awesome Tut[7], which keeps our examples compiling correctly.

---

[5]https://github.com/underscoreio/shapeless-guide/graphs/contributors
[6]https://github.com/fommil/shapeless-for-mortals
[7]https://github.com/tpolecat/tut

Part I

Type class derivation

Chapter 2

Algebraic data types and generic representations

The main idea behind generic programming is to solve problems for a wide variety of types by writing a small amount of generic code. Shapeless provides two sets of tools to this end:

1. a set of generic data types that can be inspected, traversed, and manipulated at the type level;

2. automatic mapping between *algebraic data types (ADTs)* (encoded in Scala as case classes and sealed traits) and these generic representations.

In this chapter we will start with a recap of the theory of algebraic data types and why they might be familiar to Scala developers. Then we will look at generic representations used by shapeless and discuss how they map on to concrete ADTs. Finally, we will introduce a type class called Generic that provides automatic mapping back and forth between ADTs and generic representations. We will finish with some simple examples using Generic to convert values from one type to another.

2.1   Recap: algebraic data types

Algebraic data types (ADTs)[1] are a functional programming concept with a fancy name but a very simple meaning. They are an idiomatic way of representing data using "ands" and "ors". For example:

- a shape is a rectangle **or** a circle
- a rectangle has a width **and** a height
- a circle has a radius

In ADT terminology, "and" types such as rectangle and circle are called *products* and "or" types such as shape are called *coproducts*. In Scala we typically represent products using case classes and coproducts using sealed traits:

```scala
sealed trait Shape
final case class Rectangle(width: Double, height: Double) extends Shape
final case class Circle(radius: Double) extends Shape

val rect: Shape = Rectangle(3.0, 4.0)
val circ: Shape = Circle(1.0)
```

The beauty of ADTs is that they are completely type safe. The compiler has complete knowledge of the algebras[2] we define, so it can help us write complete, correctly typed methods involving our types:

```scala
def area(shape: Shape): Double =
  shape match {
    case Rectangle(w, h) => w * h
    case Circle(r)       => math.Pi * r * r
  }

area(rect)
// res1: Double = 12.0
```

---

[1]Not to be confused with "abstract data types", which are a different tool from computer science that has little bearing on the discussion here.

[2]The word "algebra" meaning: the symbols we define, such as rectangle and circle; and the rules for manipulating those symbols, encoded as methods.

```
area(circ)
// res2: Double = 3.141592653589793
```

2.1.1   Alternative encodings

Sealed traits and case classes are undoubtedly the most convenient encoding of ADTs in Scala. However, they aren't the *only* encoding. For example, the Scala standard library provides generic products in the form of Tuples and a generic coproduct in the form of Either. We could have chosen these to encode our Shape:

```
type Rectangle2 = (Double, Double)
type Circle2    = Double
type Shape2     = Either[Rectangle2, Circle2]

val rect2: Shape2 = Left((3.0, 4.0))
val circ2: Shape2 = Right(1.0)
```

While this encoding is less readable than the case class encoding above, it does have some of the same desirable properties. We can still write completely type safe operations involving Shape2:

```
def area2(shape: Shape2): Double =
  shape match {
    case Left((w, h)) => w * h
    case Right(r)     => math.Pi * r * r
  }

area2(rect2)
// res4: Double = 12.0

area2(circ2)
// res5: Double = 3.141592653589793
```

Importantly, Shape2 is a more *generic* encoding than Shape[3]. Any code that operates on a pair of Doubles will be able to operate on a Rectangle2 and vice

---

[3]We're using "generic" in an informal way here, rather than the conventional meaning of "a type with a type parameter".

versa. As Scala developers we tend to prefer semantic types like `Rectangle` and `Circle` to generic ones like `Rectangle2` and `Circle2` precisely because of their specialised nature. However, in some cases generality is desirable. For example, if we're serializing data to disk, we don't care about the difference between a pair of `Doubles` and a `Rectangle2`. We just write two numbers and we're done.

Shapeless gives us the best of both worlds: we can use friendly semantic types by default and switch to generic representations when we want interoperability (more on this later). However, instead of using `Tuples` and `Either`, shapeless uses its own data types to represent generic products and coproducts. We'll introduce these types in the next sections.

2.2   Generic product encodings

In the previous section we introduced tuples as a generic representation of products. Unfortunately, Scala's built-in tuples have a couple of disadvantages that make them unsuitable for shapeless' purposes:

1. Each size of tuple has a different, unrelated type, making it difficult to write code that abstracts over sizes.

2. There is no type for zero-length tuples, which are important for representing products with zero fields. We could arguably use `Unit`, but we ideally want all generic representations to have a sensible common supertype. The least upper bound of `Unit` and `Tuple2` is `Any` so a combination of the two is impractical.

For these reasons, shapeless uses a different generic encoding for product types called *heterogeneous lists* or `HLists`[4].

An `HList` is either the empty list `HNil`, or a pair `::[H, T]` where H is an arbitrary type and T is another `HList`. Because every `::` has its own H and T, the type of each element is encoded separately in the type of the overall list:

---

[4]`Product` is perhaps a better name for `HList`, but the standard library unfortunately already has a type `scala.Product`.

```
import shapeless.{HList, ::, HNil}

val product: String :: Int :: Boolean :: HNil =
  "Sunday" :: 1 :: false :: HNil
```

The type and value of the HList above mirror one another. Both represent three members: a String, an Int, and a Boolean. We can retrieve the head and tail and the types of the elements are preserved:

```
val first = product.head
// first: String = Sunday

val second = product.tail.head
// second: Int = 1

val rest = product.tail.tail
// rest: Boolean :: shapeless.HNil = false :: HNil
```

The compiler knows the exact length of each HList, so it becomes a compilation error to take the head or tail of an empty list:

```
product.tail.tail.tail.head
// <console>:15: error: could not find implicit value for parameter c:
//     shapeless.ops.hlist.IsHCons[shapeless.HNil]
//         product.tail.tail.tail.head
//                               ^
```

We can manipulate and transform HLists in addition to being able to inspect and traverse them. For example, we can prepend an element with the :: method. Again, notice how the type of the result reflects the number and types of its elements:

```
val newProduct = 42L :: product
```

Shapeless also provides tools for performing more complex operations such as mapping, filtering, and concatenating lists. We'll discuss these in more detail in Part II.

The behaviour we get from HLists isn't magic. We could have achieved all of this functionality using (A, B) and Unit as alternatives to :: and HNil. However, there is an advantage in keeping our representation types separate from the semantic types used in our applications. HList provides this separation.

2.2.1   Switching representations using *Generic*

Shapeless provides a type class called Generic that allows us to switch back and forth between a concrete ADT and its generic representation. Some behind-the-scenes macro magic allows us to summon instances of Generic without boilerplate:

```scala
import shapeless.Generic

case class IceCream(name: String, numCherries: Int, inCone: Boolean)

val iceCreamGen = Generic[IceCream]
// iceCreamGen: shapeless.Generic[IceCream]{type Repr = String :: Int ::
      Boolean :: shapeless.HNil} = anon$macro$4$1@7990b7e8
```

Note that the instance of Generic has a type member Repr containing the type of its generic representation. In this case iceCreamGen.Repr is String :: Int :: Boolean :: HNil. Instances of Generic have two methods: one for converting to the Repr type and one for converting from it:

```scala
val iceCream = IceCream("Sundae", 1, false)
// iceCream: IceCream = IceCream(Sundae,1,false)

val repr = iceCreamGen.to(iceCream)
// repr: iceCreamGen.Repr = Sundae :: 1 :: false :: HNil

val iceCream2 = iceCreamGen.from(repr)
// iceCream2: IceCream = IceCream(Sundae,1,false)
```

If two ADTs have the same Repr, we can convert back and forth between them using their Generics:

```scala
case class Employee(name: String, number: Int, manager: Boolean)

// Create an employee from an ice cream:
val employee = Generic[Employee].from(Generic[IceCream].to(iceCream))
// employee: Employee = Employee(Sundae,1,false)
```

Other product types

It's worth noting that Scala tuples are actually case classes, so Generic works with them just fine:

```scala
val tupleGen = Generic[(String, Int, Boolean)]

tupleGen.to(("Hello", 123, true))
// res4: tupleGen.Repr = Hello :: 123 :: true :: HNil

tupleGen.from("Hello" :: 123 :: true :: HNil)
// res5: (String, Int, Boolean) = (Hello,123,true)
```

It also works with case classes of more than 22 fields:

```scala
case class BigData(
  a:Int,b:Int,c:Int,d:Int,e:Int,f:Int,g:Int,h:Int,i:Int,j:Int,
  k:Int,l:Int,m:Int,n:Int,o:Int,p:Int,q:Int,r:Int,s:Int,t:Int,
  u:Int,v:Int,w:Int)

Generic[BigData].from(Generic[BigData].to(BigData(
  1,2,3,4,5,6,7,8,9,10,11,12,13,14,15,16,17,18,19,20,21,22,23)))
// res6: BigData = BigData
//    (1,2,3,4,5,6,7,8,9,10,11,12,13,14,15,16,17,18,19,20,21,22,23)
```

2.3 Generic coproducts

Now we know how shapeless encodes product types. What about coproducts? We looked at Either earlier but that suffers from similar drawbacks to tuples. Again, shapeless provides its own encoding that is similar to HList:

```scala
import shapeless.{Coproduct, :+:, CNil, Inl, Inr}

case class Red()
case class Amber()
case class Green()

type Light = Red :+: Amber :+: Green :+: CNil
```

In general coproducts take the form A :+: B :+: C :+: CNil meaning "A or B or C", where :+: can be loosely interpreted as Either. The overall type of a coproduct encodes all the possible types in the disjunction, but each concrete instance contains a value for just one of the possibilities. :+: has two subtypes, Inl and Inr, that correspond loosely to Left and Right. We create instances of a coproduct by nesting Inl and Inr constructors:

```scala
val red: Light = Inl(Red())
// red: Light = Inl(Red())

val green: Light = Inr(Inr(Inl(Green())))
// green: Light = Inr(Inr(Inl(Green())))
```

Every coproduct type is terminated with CNil, which is an empty type with no values, similar to Nothing. We can't instantiate CNil or build a Coproduct purely from instances of Inr. We always have exactly one Inl in a value.

Again, it's worth stating that Coproducts aren't particularly special. The functionality above can be achieved using Either and Nothing in place of :+: and CNil. There are technical difficulties with using Nothing, but we could have used any other uninhabited or arbitrary singleton type in place of CNil.

2.3.1   Switching encodings using *Generic*

Coproduct types are difficult to parse on first glance. However, we can see how they fit into the larger picture of generic encodings. In addition to understanding case classes and case objects, shapeless' Generic type class also understands sealed traits and abstract classes:

```
import shapeless.Generic

sealed trait Shape
final case class Rectangle(width: Double, height: Double) extends Shape
final case class Circle(radius: Double) extends Shape

val gen = Generic[Shape]
// gen: shapeless.Generic[Shape]{type Repr = Rectangle :+: Circle :+:
    shapeless.CNil} = anon$macro$1$1@54c5ea24
```

The Repr of the Generic for Shape is a Coproduct of the subtypes of the
sealed trait: Rectangle :+: Circle :+: CNil. We can use the to and
from methods of the generic to map back and forth between Shape and
gen.Repr:

```
gen.to(Rectangle(3.0, 4.0))
// res3: gen.Repr = Inl(Rectangle(3.0,4.0))

gen.to(Circle(1.0))
// res4: gen.Repr = Inr(Inl(Circle(1.0)))
```

2.4 Summary

In this chapter we discussed the generic representations shapeless provides
for algebraic data types in Scala: HLists for product types and Coproducts
for coproduct types. We also introduced the Generic type class to map back
and forth between concrete ADTs and their generic representations. We
haven't yet discussed why generic encodings are so attractive. The one use
case we did cover—converting between ADTs—is fun but not tremendously
useful.

The real power of HLists and Coproducts comes from their recursive structure. We can write code to traverse representations and calculate values from
their constituent elements. In the next chapter we will look at our first real use
case: automatically deriving type class instances.

Chapter 3

Automatically deriving type class instances

In the last chapter we saw how the `Generic` type class allowed us to convert any instance of an ADT to a generic encoding made of `HLists` and `Coproducts`. In this chapter we will look at our first serious use case: automatic derivation of type class instances.

3.1   Recap: type classes

Before we get into the depths of instance derivation, let's quickly recap on the important aspects of type classes.

Type classes are a programming pattern borrowed from Haskell (the word "class" has nothing to do with classes in object oriented programming). We encode them in Scala using traits and implicits. A *type class* is a parameterised trait representing some sort of general functionality that we would like to apply to a wide range of types:

```
// Turn a value of type A into a row of cells in a CSV file:
trait CsvEncoder[A] {
```

```scala
  def encode(value: A): List[String]
}
```

We implement our type class with *instances* for each type we care about. If we want the instances to automatically be in scope we can place them in the type class' companion object. Otherwise we can place them in a separate library object for the user to import manually:

```scala
// Custom data type:
case class Employee(name: String, number: Int, manager: Boolean)

// CsvEncoder instance for the custom data type:
implicit val employeeEncoder: CsvEncoder[Employee] =
  new CsvEncoder[Employee] {
    def encode(e: Employee): List[String] =
      List(
        e.name,
        e.number.toString,
        if(e.manager) "yes" else "no"
      )
  }
```

We mark each instance with the keyword `implicit`, and define one or more entry point methods that accept an implicit parameter of the corresponding type:

```scala
def writeCsv[A](values: List[A])(implicit enc: CsvEncoder[A]): String =
  values.map(value => enc.encode(value).mkString(",")).mkString("\n")
```

We'll test `writeCsv` with some test data:

```scala
val employees: List[Employee] = List(
  Employee("Bill", 1, true),
  Employee("Peter", 2, false),
  Employee("Milton", 3, false)
)
```

When we call `writeCsv`, the compiler calculates the value of the type parameter and searches for an implicit `CsvEncoder` of the corresponding type:

```
writeCsv(employees)
// res4: String =
// Bill,1,yes
// Peter,2,no
// Milton,3,no
```

We can use `writeCsv` with any data type we like, provided we have a corresponding implicit `CsvEncoder` in scope:

```
case class IceCream(name: String, numCherries: Int, inCone: Boolean)

implicit val iceCreamEncoder: CsvEncoder[IceCream] =
  new CsvEncoder[IceCream] {
    def encode(i: IceCream): List[String] =
      List(
        i.name,
        i.numCherries.toString,
        if(i.inCone) "yes" else "no"
      )
  }

val iceCreams: List[IceCream] = List(
  IceCream("Sundae", 1, false),
  IceCream("Cornetto", 0, true),
  IceCream("Banana Split", 0, false)
)

writeCsv(iceCreams)
// res7: String =
// Sundae,1,no
// Cornetto,0,yes
// Banana Split,0,no
```

3.1.1 Resolving instances

Type classes are very flexible but they require us to define instances for every type we care about. Fortunately, the Scala compiler has a few tricks up its sleeve to resolve instances for us given sets of user-defined rules. For example, we can write a rule that creates a `CsvEncoder` for `(A, B)` given `CsvEncoders` for A and B:

```scala
implicit def pairEncoder[A, B](
  implicit
  aEncoder: CsvEncoder[A],
  bEncoder: CsvEncoder[B]
): CsvEncoder[(A, B)] =
  new CsvEncoder[(A, B)] {
    def encode(pair: (A, B)): List[String] = {
      val (a, b) = pair
      aEncoder.encode(a) ++ bEncoder.encode(b)
    }
  }
```

When all the parameters to an `implicit def` are themselves marked as `implicit`, the compiler can use it as a resolution rule to create instances from other instances. For example, if we call `writeCsv` and pass in a `List[(Employee, IceCream)]`, the compiler is able to combine `pairEncoder`, `employeeEncoder`, and `iceCreamEncoder` to produce the required `CsvEncoder[(Employee, IceCream)]`:

```scala
writeCsv(employees zip iceCreams)
// res8: String =
// Bill,1,yes,Sundae,1,no
// Peter,2,no,Cornetto,0,yes
// Milton,3,no,Banana Split,0,no
```

Given a set of rules encoded as `implicit vals` and `implicit defs`, the compiler is capable of *searching* for combinations to give it the required instances. This behaviour, known as "implicit resolution", is what makes the type class pattern so powerful in Scala.

Even with this power, the compiler can't pull apart our case classes and sealed traits. We are required to define instances for ADTs by hand. Shapeless' generic representations change all of this, allowing us to derive instances for any ADT for free.

3.1.2   Idiomatic type class definitions

The commonly accepted idiomatic style for type class definitions includes a companion object containing some standard methods:

```scala
object CsvEncoder {
  // "Summoner" method
  def apply[A](implicit enc: CsvEncoder[A]): CsvEncoder[A] =
    enc

  // "Constructor" method
  def instance[A](func: A => List[String]): CsvEncoder[A] =
    new CsvEncoder[A] {
      def encode(value: A): List[String] =
        func(value)
    }

  // Globally visible type class instances
}
```

The apply method, known as a "summoner" or "materializer", allows us to summon a type class instance given a target type:

```scala
CsvEncoder[IceCream]
// res9: CsvEncoder[IceCream] = $anon$1@4ee1e47f
```

In simple cases the summoner does the same job as the implicitly method defined in scala.Predef:

```scala
implicitly[CsvEncoder[IceCream]]
// res10: CsvEncoder[IceCream] = $anon$1@4ee1e47f
```

However, as we will see in Section 4.2, when working with shapeless we encounter situations where implicitly doesn't infer types correctly. We can always define the summoner method to do the right thing, so it's worth writing one for every type class we create. We can also use a special method from shapeless called "the" (more on this later):

```scala
import shapeless._

the[CsvEncoder[IceCream]]
// res11: CsvEncoder[IceCream] = $anon$1@4ee1e47f
```

The instance method, sometimes named pure, provides a terse syntax for creating new type class instances, reducing the boilerplate of anonymous class syntax:

```scala
implicit val booleanEncoder: CsvEncoder[Boolean] =
  new CsvEncoder[Boolean] {
    def encode(b: Boolean): List[String] =
      if(b) List("yes") else List("no")
  }
```

down to something much shorter:

```scala
implicit val booleanEncoder: CsvEncoder[Boolean] =
  instance(b => if(b) List("yes") else List("no"))
```

Unfortunately, several limitations of typesetting code in a book prevent us writing long singletons containing lots of methods and instances. We therefore tend to describe definitions outside of their context in the companion object. Bear this in mind as you read and check the accompanying repo linked in Section 1.2 for complete worked examples.

3.2   Deriving instances for products

In this section we're going to use shapeless to derive type class instances for product types (i.e. case classes). We'll use two intuitions:

1. If we have type class instances for the head and tail of an `HList`, we can derive an instance for the whole `HList`.

2. If we have a case class `A`, a `Generic[A]`, and a type class instance for the generic's `Repr`, we can combine them to create an instance for `A`.

Take `CsvEncoder` and `IceCream` as examples:

- `IceCream` has a generic `Repr` of type `String :: Int :: Boolean :: HNil`.

- The Repr is made up of a String, an Int, a Boolean, and an HNil. If we have CsvEncoders for these types, we can create an encoder for the whole thing.

- If we can derive a CsvEncoder for the Repr, we can create one for IceCream.

3.2.1   Instances for *HLists*

Let's start by defining an instance constructor and CsvEncoders for String, Int, and Boolean:

```
def createEncoder[A](func: A => List[String]): CsvEncoder[A] =
  new CsvEncoder[A] {
    def encode(value: A): List[String] = func(value)
  }

implicit val stringEncoder: CsvEncoder[String] =
  createEncoder(str => List(str))

implicit val intEncoder: CsvEncoder[Int] =
  createEncoder(num => List(num.toString))

implicit val booleanEncoder: CsvEncoder[Boolean] =
  createEncoder(bool => List(if(bool) "yes" else "no"))
```

We can combine these building blocks to create an encoder for our HList. We'll use two rules: one for HNil and one for :: as shown below:

```
import shapeless.{HList, ::, HNil}

implicit val hnilEncoder: CsvEncoder[HNil] =
  createEncoder(hnil => Nil)

implicit def hlistEncoder[H, T <: HList](
  implicit
  hEncoder: CsvEncoder[H],
  tEncoder: CsvEncoder[T]
): CsvEncoder[H :: T] =
```

```
createEncoder {
  case h :: t =>
    hEncoder.encode(h) ++ tEncoder.encode(t)
}
```

Taken together, these five instances allow us to summon `CsvEncoder`s for any `HList` involving `String`s, `Int`s, and `Boolean`s:

```
val reprEncoder: CsvEncoder[String :: Int :: Boolean :: HNil] =
  implicitly

reprEncoder.encode("abc" :: 123 :: true :: HNil)
// res9: List[String] = List(abc, 123, yes)
```

3.2.2　Instances for concrete products

We can combine our derivation rules for `HList`s with an instance of `Generic` to produce a `CsvEncoder` for `IceCream`:

```
import shapeless.Generic

implicit val iceCreamEncoder: CsvEncoder[IceCream] = {
  val gen = Generic[IceCream]
  val enc = CsvEncoder[gen.Repr]
  createEncoder(iceCream => enc.encode(gen.to(iceCream)))
}
```

and use it as follows:

```
writeCsv(iceCreams)
// res11: String =
// Sundae,1,no
// Cornetto,0,yes
// Banana Split,0,no
```

This solution is specific to `IceCream`. Ideally we'd like to have a single rule that handles all case classes that have a `Generic` and a matching `CsvEncoder`. Let's work through the derivation step by step. Here's a first cut:

```scala
implicit def genericEncoder[A](
  implicit
  gen: Generic[A],
  enc: CsvEncoder[???]
): CsvEncoder[A] = createEncoder(a => enc.encode(gen.to(a)))
```

The first problem we have is selecting a type to put in place of the ???. We want to write the Repr type associated with gen, but we can't do this:

```scala
implicit def genericEncoder[A](
  implicit
  gen: Generic[A],
  enc: CsvEncoder[gen.Repr]
): CsvEncoder[A] =
  createEncoder(a => enc.encode(gen.to(a)))
// <console>:24: error: illegal dependent method type: parameter may
//     only be referenced in a subsequent parameter section
//          gen: Generic[A],
//               ^
```

The problem here is a scoping issue: we can't refer to a type member of one parameter from another parameter in the same block. The trick to solving this is to introduce a new type parameter to our method and refer to it in each of the associated value parameters:

```scala
implicit def genericEncoder[A, R](
  implicit
  gen: Generic[A] { type Repr = R },
  enc: CsvEncoder[R]
): CsvEncoder[A] =
  createEncoder(a => enc.encode(gen.to(a)))
```

We'll cover this coding style in more detail the next chapter. Suffice to say, this definition now compiles and works as expected and we can use it with any case class as expected. Intuitively, this definition says:

> Given a type A and an HList type R, an implicit Generic to map A to R, and a CsvEncoder for R, create a CsvEncoder for A.

We now have a complete system that handles any case class. The compiler expands a call like:

```
writeCsv(iceCreams)
```

to use our family of derivation rules:

```
writeCsv(iceCreams)(
  genericEncoder(
    Generic[IceCream],
    hlistEncoder(stringEncoder,
      hlistEncoder(intEncoder,
        hlistEncoder(booleanEncoder, hnilEncoder)))))
```

and can infer the correct expansions for many different product types. I'm sure you'll agree, it's nice not to have to write this code by hand!

Aux type aliases

Type refinements like `Generic[A] { type Repr = L }` are verbose and difficult to read, so shapeless provides a type alias `Generic.Aux` to rephrase the type member as a type parameter:

```
package shapeless

object Generic {
  type Aux[A, R] = Generic[A] { type Repr = R }
}
```

Using this alias we get a much more readable definition:

```
implicit def genericEncoder[A, R](
  implicit
  gen: Generic.Aux[A, R],
  env: CsvEncoder[R]
): CsvEncoder[A] =
  createEncoder(a => env.encode(gen.to(a)))
```

> Note that the Aux type isn't changing any semantics—it's just making things easier to read. This "Aux pattern" is used frequently in the shapeless codebase.

3.2.3   So what are the downsides?

If all of the above seems pretty magical, allow us to provide one significant dose of reality. If things go wrong, the compiler isn't great at telling us why.

There are two main reasons the code above might fail to compile. The first is when the compiler can't find an instance of Generic. For example, here we try to call writeCsv with a non-case class:

```
class Foo(bar: String, baz: Int)

writeCsv(List(new Foo("abc", 123)))
// <console>:26: error: could not find implicit value for parameter
     encoder: CsvEncoder[Foo]
//         writeCsv(List(new Foo("abc", 123)))
//                    ^
```

In this case the error message is relatively easy to understand. If shapeless can't calculate a Generic it means that the type in question isn't an ADT— somewhere in the algebra there is a type that isn't a case class or a sealed abstract type.

The other potential source of failure is when the compiler can't calculate a CsvEncoder for our HList. This normally happens because we don't have an encoder for one of the fields in our ADT. For example, we haven't yet defined a CsvEncoder for java.util.Date, so the following code fails:

```
import java.util.Date

case class Booking(room: String, date: Date)

writeCsv(List(Booking("Lecture hall", new Date())))
// <console>:28: error: could not find implicit value for parameter
     encoder: CsvEncoder[Booking]
```

```
//          writeCsv(List(Booking("Lecture hall", new Date())))
//                   ^
```

The message we get here isn't very helpful. All the compiler knows is it tried a lot of combinations of implicits and couldn't make them work. It has no idea which combination came closest to the desired result, so it can't tell us where the source(s) of failure lie.

There's not much good news here. We have to find the source of the error ourselves by a process of elimination. We'll discuss debugging techniques in Section 3.5. For now, the main redeeming feature is that implicit resolution always fails at compile time. There's little chance that we will end up with code that fails during execution.

3.3 Deriving instances for coproducts

In the last section we created a set of rules to automatically derive a CsvEncoder for any product type. In this section we will apply the same patterns to coproducts. Let's return to our shape ADT as an example:

```scala
sealed trait Shape
final case class Rectangle(width: Double, height: Double) extends Shape
final case class Circle(radius: Double) extends Shape
```

The generic representation for Shape is Rectangle :+: Circle :+: CNil. In Section 3.2.2 we defined product encoders for Rectangle and Circle. Now, to write generic CsvEncoders for :+: and CNil, we can use the same principles we used for HLists:

```scala
import shapeless.{Coproduct, :+:, CNil, Inl, Inr}

implicit val cnilEncoder: CsvEncoder[CNil] =
  createEncoder(cnil => throw new Exception("Inconceivable!"))

implicit def coproductEncoder[H, T <: Coproduct](
  implicit
  hEncoder: CsvEncoder[H],
```

```
    tEncoder: CsvEncoder[T]
  ): CsvEncoder[H :+: T] = createEncoder {
    case Inl(h) => hEncoder.encode(h)
    case Inr(t) => tEncoder.encode(t)
  }
```

There are two key points of note:

1. Because Coproducts are *disjunctions* of types, the encoder for :+: has to *choose* whether to encode a left or right value. We pattern match on the two subtypes of :+:, which are Inl for left and Inr for right.

2. Alarmingly, the encoder for CNil throws an exception! Don't panic, though. Remember that we can't create values of type CNil, so the throw expression is dead code. It's ok to fail abruptly here because we will never reach this point.

If we place these definitions alongside our product encoders from Section 3.2, we should be able to serialize a list of shapes. Let's give it a try:

```
val shapes: List[Shape] = List(
  Rectangle(3.0, 4.0),
  Circle(1.0)
)

writeCsv(shapes)
// <console>:26: error: could not find implicit value for parameter
      encoder: CsvEncoder[Shape]
//         writeCsv(shapes)
//                 ^
```

Oh no, it failed! The error message is unhelpful as we discussed earlier. The reason for the failure is we don't have a CsvEncoder instance for Double:

```
implicit val doubleEncoder: CsvEncoder[Double] =
  createEncoder(d => List(d.toString))
```

With this definition in place, everything works as expected:

```
writeCsv(shapes)
// res7: String =
// 3.0,4.0
// 1.0
```

> *SI-7046 and you*
>
> There is a Scala compiler bug called SI-7046[a] that can cause coproduct
> generic resolution to fail. The bug causes certain parts of the macro
> API, on which shapeless depends, to be sensitive to the order of the
> definitions in our source code. Problems can often be worked around
> by reordering code and renaming files, but such workarounds tend to
> be volatile and unreliable.
>
> If you are using Lightbend Scala 2.11.8 or earlier and coproduct resolu-
> tion fails for you, consider upgrading to Lightbend Scala 2.11.9 or Type-
> level Scala 2.11.8. SI-7046 is fixed in each of these releases.
>
> ───────────────
> [a]https://issues.scala-lang.org/browse/SI-7046

3.3.1   Aligning CSV output

Our CSV encoder isn't very practical in its current form. It allows fields from
Rectangle and Circle to occupy the same columns in the output. To fix this
problem we need to modify the definition of CsvEncoder to incorporate the
width of the data type and space the output accordingly. The examples repo
linked in Section 1.2 contains a complete implementation of CsvEncoder that
addresses this problem.

3.4   Deriving instances for recursive types

Let's try something more ambitious—a binary tree:

```scala
sealed trait Tree[A]
case class Branch[A](left: Tree[A], right: Tree[A]) extends Tree[A]
case class Leaf[A](value: A) extends Tree[A]
```

Theoretically we should already have all of the definitions in place to summon a CSV writer for this definition. However, calls to `writeCsv` fail to compile:

```scala
CsvEncoder[Tree[Int]]
// <console>:23: error: could not find implicit value for parameter enc:
//        CsvEncoder[Tree[Int]]
//         CsvEncoder[Tree[Int]]
//                    ^
```

The problem is that our type is recursive. The compiler senses an infinite loop applying our implicits and gives up.

3.4.1 Implicit divergence

Implicit resolution is a search process. The compiler uses heuristics to determine whether it is "converging" on a solution. If the heuristics don't yield favorable results for a particular branch of search, the compiler assumes the branch is not converging and moves onto another.

One heuristic is specifically designed to avoid infinite loops. If the compiler sees the same target type twice in a particular branch of search, it gives up and moves on. We can see this happening if we look at the expansion for `CsvEncoder[Tree[Int]]` The implicit resolution process goes through the following types:

```scala
CsvEncoder[Tree[Int]]                            // 1
CsvEncoder[Branch[Int] :+: Leaf[Int] :+: CNil]   // 2
CsvEncoder[Branch[Int]]                          // 3
CsvEncoder[Tree[Int] :: Tree[Int] :: HNil]       // 4
CsvEncoder[Tree[Int]]                            // 5 uh oh
```

We see `Tree[A]` twice in lines 1 and 5, so the compiler moves onto another branch of search. The eventual consequence is that it fails to find a suitable implicit.

In fact, the situation is worse than this. If the compiler sees the same type constructor twice and the complexity of the type parameters is *increasing*, it assumes that branch of search is "diverging". This is a problem for shapeless because types like ::[H, T] and :+:[H, T] can appear several times as the compiler expands different generic representations. This causes the compiler to give up prematurely even though it would eventually find a solution if it persisted with the same expansion. Consider the following types:

```
case class Bar(baz: Int, qux: String)
case class Foo(bar: Bar)
```

The expansion for Foo looks like this:

```
CsvEncoder[Foo]                    // 1
CsvEncoder[Bar :: HNil]            // 2
CsvEncoder[Bar]                    // 3
CsvEncoder[Int :: String :: HNil] // 4 uh oh
```

The compiler attempts to resolve a CsvEncoder[::[H, T]] twice in this branch of search, on lines 2 and 4. The type parameter for T is more complex on line 4 than on line 2, so the compiler assumes (incorrectly in this case) that the branch of search is diverging. It moves onto another branch and, again, the result is failure to generate a suitable instance.

3.4.2 *Lazy*

Implicit divergence would be a show-stopper for libraries like shapeless. Fortunately, shapeless provides a type called Lazy as a workaround. Lazy does two things:

1. it suppresses implicit divergence at compile time by guarding against the aforementioned over-defensive convergence heuristics;

2. it defers evaluation of the implicit parameter at runtime, permitting the derivation of self-referential implicits.

We use Lazy by wrapping it around specific implicit parameters. As a rule of thumb, it is always a good idea to wrap the "head" parameter of any HList or Coproduct rule and the Repr parameter of any Generic rule in Lazy:

```
implicit def hlistEncoder[H, T <: HList](
  implicit
  hEncoder: Lazy[CsvEncoder[H]], // wrap in Lazy
  tEncoder: CsvEncoder[T]
): CsvEncoder[H :: T] = createEncoder {
  case h :: t =>
    hEncoder.value.encode(h) ++ tEncoder.encode(t)
}

implicit def coproductEncoder[H, T <: Coproduct](
  implicit
  hEncoder: Lazy[CsvEncoder[H]], // wrap in Lazy
  tEncoder: CsvEncoder[T]
): CsvEncoder[H :+: T] = createEncoder {
  case Inl(h) => hEncoder.value.encode(h)
  case Inr(t) => tEncoder.encode(t)
}

implicit def genericEncoder[A, R](
  implicit
  gen: Generic.Aux[A, R],
  rEncoder: Lazy[CsvEncoder[R]] // wrap in Lazy
): CsvEncoder[A] = createEncoder { value =>
  rEncoder.value.encode(gen.to(value))
}
```

This prevents the compiler giving up prematurely, and enables the solution to work on complex/recursive types like Tree:

```
CsvEncoder[Tree[Int]]
// res2: CsvEncoder[Tree[Int]] = $anon$1@56ac989a
```

3.5   Debugging implicit resolution

Failures in implicit resolution can be confusing and frustrating. Here are a couple of techniques to use when implicits go bad.

3.5.1   Debugging using *implicitly*

What can we do when the compiler simply fails to find an implicit value? The
failure could be caused by the resolution of any one of the implicits in use. For
example:

```
case class Foo(bar: Int, baz: Float)

CsvEncoder[Foo]
// <console>:29: error: could not find implicit value for parameter enc:
      CsvEncoder[Foo]
//          CsvEncoder[Foo]
//                    ^
```

The reason for the failure is that we haven't defined a CsvEncoder for Float.
However, this may not be obvious in application code. We can work through
the expected expansion sequence to find the source of the error, inserting calls
to CsvEncoder.apply or implicitly above the error to see if they compile.
We start with the generic representation of Foo:

```
CsvEncoder[Int :: Float :: HNil]
// <console>:27: error: could not find implicit value for parameter enc:
      CsvEncoder[Int :: Float :: shapeless.HNil]
//          CsvEncoder[Int :: Float :: HNil]
//                    ^
```

This fails so we know we have to search deeper in the expansion. The next
step is to try the components of the HList:

```
CsvEncoder[Int]

CsvEncoder[Float]
// <console>:27: error: could not find implicit value for parameter enc:
      CsvEncoder[Float]
//          CsvEncoder[Float]
//                    ^
```

Int passes but Float fails. CsvEncoder[Float] is a leaf in our tree of expansions, so we know to start by implementing this missing instance. If adding

the instance doesn't fix the problem we repeat the process to find the next point of failure.

3.5.2   Debugging using *reify*

The reify method from scala.reflect takes a Scala expression as a parameter and returns an AST object representing the expression tree, complete with type annotations:

```
import scala.reflect.runtime.universe._

println(reify(CsvEncoder[Int]))
// Expr[CsvEncoder[Int]]($read.$iw.$iw.$iw.CsvEncoder.apply[Int](
    $read.$iw.$iw.$iw.intEncoder))
```

The types inferred during implicit resolution can give us hints about problems. After implicit resolution, any remaining existential types such as A or T provide a sign that something has gone wrong. Similarly, "top" and "bottom" types such as Any and Nothing are evidence of failure.

3.6   Summary

In this chapter we discussed how to use Generic, HLists, and Coproducts to automatically derive type class instances. We also covered the Lazy type as a means of handling complex/recursive types. Taking all of this into account, we can write a common skeleton for deriving type class instances as follows.

First, define the type class:

```
trait MyTC[A]
```

Define primitive instances:

```scala
implicit def intInstance: MyTC[Int] = ???
implicit def stringInstance: MyTC[String] = ???
implicit def booleanInstance: MyTC[Boolean] = ???
```

Define instances for HList:

```scala
import shapeless._

implicit def hnilInstance: MyTC[HNil] = ???

implicit def hlistInstance[H, T <: HList](
  implicit
  hInstance: Lazy[MyTC[H]], // wrap in Lazy
  tInstance: MyTC[T]
): MyTC[H :: T] = ???
```

If required, define instances for Coproduct:

```scala
implicit def cnilInstance: MyTC[CNil] = ???

implicit def coproductInstance[H, T <: Coproduct](
  implicit
  hInstance: Lazy[MyTC[H]], // wrap in Lazy
  tInstance: MyTC[T]
): MyTC[H :+: T] = ???
```

Finally, define an instance for Generic:

```scala
implicit def genericInstance[A, R](
  implicit
  generic: Generic.Aux[A, R],
  rInstance: Lazy[MyTC[R]] // wrap in Lazy
): MyTC[A] = ???
```

In the next chapter we'll cover some useful theory and programming patterns to help write code in this style. In Chapter 5 we will revisit type class derivation using a variant of Generic that allows us to inspect field and type names in our ADTs.

Chapter 4

Working with types and implicits

In the last chapter we saw one of the most compelling use cases for shapeless: automatically deriving type class instances. There are plenty of even more powerful examples coming later. However, before we move on, we should take time to discuss some theory we've skipped over and establish a set of patterns for writing and debugging type- and implicit-heavy code.

4.1 Dependent types

Last chapter we spent a lot of time using Generic, the type class for mapping ADT types to generic representations. However, we haven't yet discussed an important bit of theory that underpins Generic and much of shapeless: *dependent types*.

To illustrate this, let's take a closer look at Generic. Here's a simplified version of the definition:

```
trait Generic[A] {
  type Repr
  def to(value: A): Repr
  def from(value: Repr): A
}
```

Instances of `Generic` reference two other types: a type parameter A and a type member Repr. Suppose we implement a method getRepr as follows. What type will we get back?

```
import shapeless.Generic

def getRepr[A](value: A)(implicit gen: Generic[A]) =
  gen.to(value)
```

The answer is it depends on the instance we get for gen. In expanding the call to getRepr, the compiler will search for a Generic[A] and the result type will be whatever Repr is defined in that instance:

```
case class Vec(x: Int, y: Int)
case class Rect(origin: Vec, size: Vec)

getRepr(Vec(1, 2))
// res1: Int :: Int :: shapeless.HNil = 1 :: 2 :: HNil

getRepr(Rect(Vec(0, 0), Vec(5, 5)))
// res2: Vec :: Vec :: shapeless.HNil = Vec(0,0) :: Vec(5,5) :: HNil
```

What we're seeing here is called *dependent typing*: the result type of getRepr depends on its value parameters via their type members. Suppose we had specified Repr as type parameter on Generic instead of a type member:

```
trait Generic2[A, Repr]

def getRepr2[A, R](value: A)(implicit generic: Generic2[A, R]): R =
  ???
```

We would have had to pass the desired value of Repr to getRepr as a type parameter, effectively making getRepr useless. The intuitive take-away from this is that type parameters are useful as "inputs" and type members are useful as "outputs".

4.2 Dependently typed functions

Shapeless uses dependent types all over the place: in `Generic`, in `Witness` (which we will see in the next chapter), and in a host of other "ops" type classes that we will survey in Part II of this guide.

For example, shapeless provides a type class called `Last` that returns the last element in an `HList`. Here's a simplified version of its definition:

```
package shapeless.ops.hlist

trait Last[L <: HList] {
  type Out
  def apply(in: L): Out
}
```

We can summon instances of `Last` to inspect `HList`s in our code. In the two examples below note that the `Out` types are dependent on the `HList` types we started with:

```
import shapeless.{HList, ::, HNil}

import shapeless.ops.hlist.Last

val last1 = Last[String :: Int :: HNil]
// last1: shapeless.ops.hlist.Last[String :: Int :: shapeless.HNil]{type
     Out = Int} = shapeless.ops.hlist$Last$$anon$34@3f424e49

val last2 = Last[Int :: String :: HNil]
// last2: shapeless.ops.hlist.Last[Int :: String :: shapeless.HNil]{type
     Out = String} = shapeless.ops.hlist$Last$$anon$34@85f3f44
```

Once we have summoned instances of `Last`, we can use them at the value level via their `apply` methods:

```
last1("foo" :: 123 :: HNil)
// res1: last1.Out = 123

last2(321 :: "bar" :: HNil)
```

```
// res2: last2.Out = bar
```

We get two forms of protection against errors. The implicits defined for `Last` ensure we can only summon instances if the input `HList` has at least one element:

```
Last[HNil]
// <console>:15: error: Implicit not found: shapeless.Ops.Last[shapeless
      .HNil]. shapeless.HNil is empty, so there is no last element.
//        Last[HNil]
//              ^
```

In addition, the type parameters on the instances of `Last` check whether we pass in the expected type of `HList`:

```
last1(321 :: "bar" :: HNil)
// <console>:16: error: type mismatch;
//  found   : Int :: String :: shapeless.HNil
//  required: String :: Int :: shapeless.HNil
//        last1(321 :: "bar" :: HNil)
//              ^
```

As a further example, let's implement our own type class, called `Second`, that returns the second element in an `HList`:

```
trait Second[L <: HList] {
  type Out
  def apply(value: L): Out
}

object Second {
  type Aux[L <: HList, O] = Second[L] { type Out = O }

  def apply[L <: HList](implicit inst: Second[L]): Aux[L, inst.Out] =
    inst
}
```

This code uses the idiomatic layout described in Section 3.1.2. We define the `Aux` type in the companion object beside the standard `apply` method for summoning instances.

Summoner methods versus "implicitly" versus "the"

Note that the return type on apply is Aux[L, 0], not Second[L]. This is important. Using Aux ensures the apply method does not erase the type members on summoned instances. If we define the return type as Second[L], the Out type member will be erased from the return type and the type class will not work correctly.

The implicitly method from scala.Predef has this behaviour. Compare the type of an instance of Last summoned with implicitly:

```
implicitly[Last[String :: Int :: HNil]]
// res6: shapeless.ops.hlist.Last[String :: Int :: shapeless.HNil]
       = shapeless.ops.hlist$Last$$anon$34@534260
```

to the type of an instance summoned with Last.apply:

```
Last[String :: Int :: HNil]
// res7: shapeless.ops.hlist.Last[String :: Int :: shapeless.HNil
   ]{type Out = Int} = shapeless.ops.
   hlist$Last$$anon$34@3bbb599d
```

The type summoned by implicitly has no Out type member. For this reason, we should avoid implicitly when working with dependently typed functions. We can either use custom summoner methods, or we can use shapeless' replacement method, the:

```
import shapeless._

the[Last[String :: Int :: HNil]]
// res8: shapeless.ops.hlist.Last[String :: Int :: shapeless.HNil
   ]{type Out = Int} = shapeless.ops.
   hlist$Last$$anon$34@40c45ff5
```

We only need a single instance, defined for HLists of at least two elements:

```
implicit def hlistSecond[A, B, Rest <: HList]: Aux[A :: B :: Rest, B] =
  new Second[A :: B :: Rest] {
    type Out = B
    def apply(value: A :: B :: Rest): B =
      value.tail.head
  }
```

We can summon instances using Second.apply:

```
val second1 = Second[String :: Boolean :: Int :: HNil]
// second1: Second[String :: Boolean :: Int :: shapeless.HNil]{type Out
    = Boolean} = $anon$1@6c3ff24d

val second2 = Second[String :: Int :: Boolean :: HNil]
// second2: Second[String :: Int :: Boolean :: shapeless.HNil]{type Out
    = Int} = $anon$1@e876e11
```

Summoning is subject to similar constraints as Last. If we try to summon an instance for an incompatible HList, resolution fails and we get a compile error:

```
Second[String :: HNil]
// <console>:26: error: could not find implicit value for parameter inst
    : Second[String :: shapeless.HNil]
//         Second[String :: HNil]
//                ^
```

Summoned instances come with an apply method that operates on the relevant type of HList at the value level:

```
second1("foo" :: true :: 123 :: HNil)
// res10: second1.Out = true

second2("bar" :: 321 :: false :: HNil)
// res11: second2.Out = 321

second1("baz" :: HNil)
// <console>:27: error: type mismatch;
//  found    : String :: shapeless.HNil
//  required: String :: Boolean :: Int :: shapeless.HNil
//         second1("baz" :: HNil)
```

```
//                    ^
```

4.3 Chaining dependent functions

Dependently typed functions provide a means of calculating one type from another. We can *chain* dependently typed functions to perform calculations involving multiple steps. For example, we should be able to use a Generic to calculate a Repr for a case class, and use a Last to calculate the type of the last element. Let's try coding this:

```
def lastField[A](input: A)(
  implicit
  gen: Generic[A],
  last: Last[gen.Repr]
): last.Out = last.apply(gen.to(input))
// <console>:28: error: illegal dependent method type: parameter may
//     only be referenced in a subsequent parameter section
//          gen: Generic[A],
//              ^
```

Unfortunately our code doesn't compile. This is the same problem we had in Section 3.2.2 with our definition of genericEncoder. We worked around the problem by lifting the free type variable out as a type parameter:

```
def lastField[A, Repr <: HList](input: A)(
  implicit
  gen: Generic.Aux[A, Repr],
  last: Last[Repr]
): last.Out = last.apply(gen.to(input))

lastField(Rect(Vec(1, 2), Vec(3, 4)))
// res13: Vec = Vec(3,4)
```

As a general rule, we always write code in this style. By encoding all the free variables as type parameters, we enable the compiler to unify them with appropriate types. This goes for more subtle constraints as well. For example, suppose we wanted to summon a Generic for a case class of exactly one field. We might be tempted to write this:

```scala
def getWrappedValue[A, H](input: A)(
  implicit
  gen: Generic.Aux[A, H :: HNil]
): H = gen.to(input).head
```

The result here is more insidious. The method definition compiles but the compiler can never find implicits at the call site:

```scala
case class Wrapper(value: Int)

getWrappedValue(Wrapper(42))
// <console>:30: error: could not find implicit value for parameter gen:
//         shapeless.Generic.Aux[Wrapper,H :: shapeless.HNil]
//         getWrappedValue(Wrapper(42))
//                         ^
```

The error message hints at the problem. The clue is in the appearance of the type H. This is the name of a type parameter in the method: it shouldn't be appearing in the type the compiler is trying to unify. The problem is that the gen parameter is over-constrained: the compiler can't find a Repr *and* ensure its length at the same time. The type Nothing also often provides a clue, appearing when the compiler fails to unify covariant type parameters.

The solution to our problem above is to separate implicit resolution into steps:

1. find a Generic with a suitable Repr for A;
2. provide that the Repr has a head type H.

Here's a revised version of the method using =:= to constrain Repr:

```scala
def getWrappedValue[A, Repr <: HList, Head, Tail <: HList](input: A)(
  implicit
  gen: Generic.Aux[A, Repr],
  ev: (Head :: Tail) =:= Repr
): Head = gen.to(input).head
// <console>:30: error: could not find implicit value for parameter c:
//     shapeless.ops.hlist.IsHCons[gen.Repr]
```

```
//          ): Head = gen.to(input).head
//                                  ^
```

This doesn't compile because the head method in the method body requires an implicit parameter of type IsHCons. This is a much simpler error message to fix—we just need to learn a tool from shapeless' toolbox. IsHCons is a shapeless type class that splits an HList into a Head and Tail. We can use IsHCons instead of =:=:

```
import shapeless.ops.hlist.IsHCons

def getWrappedValue[A, Repr <: HList, Head](in: A)(
  implicit
  gen: Generic.Aux[A, Repr],
  isHCons: IsHCons.Aux[Repr, Head, HNil]
): Head = gen.to(in).head
```

This fixes the bug. Both the method definition and the call site now compile as expected:

```
getWrappedValue(Wrapper(42))
// res16: Int = 42
```

The take home point here isn't that we solved the problem using IsHCons. Shapeless provides a lot of tools like this (see Chapters 6 to 8), and we can supplement them where necessary with our own type classes. The important point is to understand the process we use to write code that compiles and is capable of finding solutions. We'll finish off this section with a step-by-step guide summarising our findings so far.

4.4 Summary

When coding with shapeless, we are often trying to find a target type that depends on values in our code. This relationship is called *dependent typing*.

Problems involving dependent types can be conveniently expressed using implicit search, allowing the compiler to resolve intermediate and target types given a starting point at the call site.

We often have to use multiple steps to calculate a result (e.g. using a `Generic` to get a `Repr`, then using another type class to get to another type). When we do this, there are a few rules we can follow to ensure our code compiles and works as expected:

1. We should extract every intermediate type out to a type parameter. Many type parameters won't be used in the result, but the compiler needs them to know which types it has to unify.

2. The compiler resolves implicits from left to right, backtracking if it can't find a working combination. We should write implicits in the order we need them, using one or more type variables to connect them to previous implicits.

3. The compiler can only solve for one constraint at a time, so we mustn't over-constrain any single implicit.

4. We should state the return type explicitly, specifying any type parameters and type members that may be needed elsewhere. Type members are often important, so we should use Aux types to preserve them where appropriate. If we don't state them in the return type, they won't be available to the compiler for further implicit resolution.

5. The Aux type alias pattern is useful for keeping code readable. We should look out for Aux aliases when using tools from the shapeless toolbox, and implement Aux aliases on our own dependently typed functions.

When we find a useful chain of dependently typed operations we can capture them as a single type class. This is sometimes called the "lemma" pattern (a term borrowed from mathematical proofs). We'll see an example of this pattern in Section 6.2.

Chapter 5

Accessing names during implicit derivation

Often, the type class instances we define need access to more than just types. In this chapter we will look at a variant of `Generic` called `LabelledGeneric` that gives us access to field names and type names.

To begin with we have some theory to cover. `LabelledGeneric` uses some clever techniques to expose name information at the type level. To understand these techniques we must discuss *literal types*, *singleton types*, *phantom types*, and *type tagging*.

5.1 Literal types

A Scala value may have multiple types. For example, the string `"hello"` has at least three types: `String`, `AnyRef`, and `Any`[1]:

---

[1] `String` also has a bunch of other types like `Serializable` and `Comparable` but let's ignore those for now.

```
"hello" : String
// res0: String = hello

"hello" : AnyRef
// res1: AnyRef = hello

"hello" : Any
// res2: Any = hello
```

Interestingly, `"hello"` also has another type: a "singleton type" that belongs exclusively to that one value. This is similar to the singleton type we get when we define a companion object:

```
object Foo

Foo
// res3: Foo.type = Foo$@75399014
```

The type Foo.type is the type of Foo, and Foo is the only value with that type.

Singleton types applied to literal values are called *literal types*. These have existed in Scala for a long time, but we don't normally interact with them because the default behaviour of the compiler is to "widen" literals to their nearest non-singleton type. For example, these two expressions are essentially equivalent:

```
"hello"
// res4: String = hello

("hello" : String)
// res5: String = hello
```

Shapeless provides a few tools for working with literal types. First, there is a `narrow` macro that converts a literal expression to a singleton-typed literal expression:

```
import shapeless.syntax.singleton._
```

```
var x = 42.narrow
// x: Int(42) = 42
```

Note the type of x here: `Int(42)` is a literal type. It is a subtype of `Int` that only contains the value 42. If we attempt to assign a different number to x, we get a compile error:

```
x = 43
// <console>:16: error: type mismatch:
//   found   : Int(43)
//   required: Int(42)
//          x = 43
//              ^
```

However, x is still an `Int` according to normal subtyping rules. If we operate on x we get a regular type of result:

```
x + 1
// res6: Int = 43
```

We can use `narrow` on any literal in Scala:

```
1.narrow
// res7: Int(1) = 1

true.narrow
// res8: Boolean(true) = true

"hello".narrow
// res9: String("hello") = hello

// and so on...
```

However, we can't use it on compound expressions:

```
math.sqrt(4).narrow
// <console>:17: error: Expression scala.math.`package`.sqrt(4.0) does
//      not evaluate to a constant or a stable reference value
//          math.sqrt(4.0).narrow
```

```
//                    ^
// <console>:17: error: value narrow is not a member of Double
//       math.sqrt(4.0).narrow
//                        ^
```

> *Literal types in Scala*
>
> Until recently, Scala had no syntax for writing literal types. The types
> were there in the compiler but we couldn't express them directly in
> code. However, as of Lightbend Scala 2.12.1, Lightbend Scala 2.11.9,
> and Typelevel Scala 2.11.8 we have direct syntax support for literal
> types. In these versions of Scala we can use the -Yliteral-types
> compiler option and write declarations like the following:
>
> ```
> val theAnswer: 42 = 42
> // theAnswer: 42 = 42
> ```
>
> The type 42 is the same as the type Int(42) we saw in printed output
> earlier. You'll still see Int(42) in output for legacy reasons, but the
> canonical syntax going forward is 42.

5.2   Type tagging and phantom types

Shapeless uses literal types to model the names of fields in case classes. It
does this by "tagging" the types of the fields with the literal types of their
names. Before we see how shapeless does this, we'll do it ourselves to show
that there's no magic (well... minimal magic, at any rate). Suppose we have a
number:

```
val number = 42
```

This number is an Int in two worlds: at runtime, where it has an actual value
and methods that we can call, and at compile-time, where the compiler uses
the type to calculate which pieces of code work together and to search for
implicits.

We can modify the type of number at compile time without modifying its run-time behaviour by "tagging" it with a "phantom type". Phantom types are types with no run-time semantics, like this:

```
trait Cherries
```

We can tag number using asInstanceOf. We end up with a value that is both an Int and a Cherries at compile-time, and an Int at run-time:

```
val numCherries = number.asInstanceOf[Int with Cherries]
// numCherries: Int with Cherries = 42
```

Shapeless uses this trick to tag fields and subtypes in an ADT with the singleton types of their names. If you find using asInstanceOf uncomfortable then don't worry: shapeless provides two tagging syntaxes to avoid such unsavoriness.

The first syntax, ->>, tags the expression on the right of the arrow with the singleton type of the literal expression on the left:

```
import shapeless.labelled.{KeyTag, FieldType}
import shapeless.syntax.singleton._

val someNumber = 123

val numCherries = "numCherries" ->> someNumber
// numCherries: Int with shapeless.labelled.KeyTag[String("numCherries")
//       ,Int] = 123
```

Here we are tagging someNumber with the following phantom type:

```
KeyTag["numCherries", Int]
```

The tag encodes both the name and type of the field, the combination of which is useful when searching for entries in a Repr using implicit resolution.

The second syntax takes the tag as a type rather than a literal value. This is useful when we know what tag to use but don't have the ability to write specific literals in our code:

```
import shapeless.labelled.field

field[Cherries](123)
// res11: shapeless.labelled.FieldType[Cherries,Int] = 123
```

FieldType is a type alias that simplifies extracting the tag and base types from a tagged type:

```
type FieldType[K, V] = V with KeyTag[K, V]
```

As we'll see in a moment, shapeless uses this mechanism to tag fields and subtypes with their names in our source code.

Tags exist purely at compile time and have no runtime representation. How do we convert them to values we can use at runtime? Shapeless provides a type class called Witness for this purpose[2]. If we combine Witness and FieldType, we get something very compelling—the ability to extract the field name from a tagged field:

```
import shapeless.Witness

val numCherries = "numCherries" ->> 123
// numCherries: Int with shapeless.labelled.KeyTag[String("numCherries")
//     ,Int] = 123

// Get the tag from a tagged value:
def getFieldName[K, V](value: FieldType[K, V])
    (implicit witness: Witness.Aux[K]): K =
  witness.value

getFieldName(numCherries)
// res13: String = numCherries

// Get the untagged type of a tagged value:
def getFieldValue[K, V](value: FieldType[K, V]): V =
  value

getFieldValue(numCherries)
```

---

[2]The term "witness" is borrowed from mathematical proofs[3].

```
// res15: Int = 123
```

If we build an HList of tagged elements, we get a data structure that has some of the properties of a Map. We can reference fields by tag, manipulate and replace them, and maintain all of the type and naming information along the way. Shapeless calls these structures "records".

5.2.1 Records and *LabelledGeneric*

Records are HLists of tagged elements:

```
import shapeless.{HList, ::, HNil}

val garfield = ("cat" ->> "Garfield") :: ("orange" ->> true) :: HNil
// garfield: String with shapeless.labelled.KeyTag[String("cat"),String]
//      :: Boolean with shapeless.labelled.KeyTag[String("orange"),Boolean]
//    ] :: shapeless.HNil = Garfield :: true :: HNil
```

For clarity, the type of garfield is as follows:

```
// FieldType["cat",    String]  ::
// FieldType["orange", Boolean] ::
// HNil
```

We don't need to go into depth regarding records here; suffice to say that records are the generic representation used by LabelledGeneric. LabelledGeneric tags each item in a product or coproduct with the corresponding field or type name from the concrete ADT (although the names are represented as Symbols, not Strings). Shapeless provides a suite of Map-like operations on records, some of which we'll cover in Section 6.4. For now, though, let's derive some type classes using LabelledGeneric.

5.3 Deriving product instances with *LabelledGeneric*

We'll use a running example of JSON encoding to illustrate LabelledGeneric. We'll define a JsonEncoder type class that converts values to a JSON AST.

This is the approach taken by Argonaut, Circe, Play JSON, Spray JSON, and many other Scala JSON libraries.

First we'll define our JSON data type:

```scala
sealed trait JsonValue
case class JsonObject(fields: List[(String, JsonValue)]) extends
    JsonValue
case class JsonArray(items: List[JsonValue]) extends JsonValue
case class JsonString(value: String) extends JsonValue
case class JsonNumber(value: Double) extends JsonValue
case class JsonBoolean(value: Boolean) extends JsonValue
case object JsonNull extends JsonValue
```

then the type class for encoding values as JSON:

```scala
trait JsonEncoder[A] {
  def encode(value: A): JsonValue
}

object JsonEncoder {
  def apply[A](implicit enc: JsonEncoder[A]): JsonEncoder[A] = enc
}
```

then a few primitive instances:

```scala
def createEncoder[A](func: A => JsonValue): JsonEncoder[A] =
  new JsonEncoder[A] {
    def encode(value: A): JsonValue = func(value)
  }

implicit val stringEncoder: JsonEncoder[String] =
  createEncoder(str => JsonString(str))

implicit val doubleEncoder: JsonEncoder[Double] =
  createEncoder(num => JsonNumber(num))

implicit val intEncoder: JsonEncoder[Int] =
  createEncoder(num => JsonNumber(num))

implicit val booleanEncoder: JsonEncoder[Boolean] =
```

```
createEncoder(bool => JsonBoolean(bool))
```

and a few instance combinators:

```
implicit def listEncoder[A]
    (implicit enc: JsonEncoder[A]): JsonEncoder[List[A]] =
  createEncoder(list => JsonArray(list.map(enc.encode)))

implicit def optionEncoder[A]
    (implicit enc: JsonEncoder[A]): JsonEncoder[Option[A]] =
  createEncoder(opt => opt.map(enc.encode).getOrElse(JsonNull))
```

Ideally, when we encode ADTs as JSON, we would like to use the correct field names in the output JSON:

```
case class IceCream(name: String, numCherries: Int, inCone: Boolean)

val iceCream = IceCream("Sundae", 1, false)

// Ideally we'd like to produce something like this:
val iceCreamJson: JsonValue =
  JsonObject(List(
    "name"       -> JsonString("Sundae"),
    "numCherries" -> JsonNumber(1),
    "inCone"     -> JsonBoolean(false)
  ))
```

This is where `LabelledGeneric` comes in. Let's summon an instance for `IceCream` and see what kind of representation it produces:

```
import shapeless.LabelledGeneric

val gen = LabelledGeneric[IceCream].to(iceCream)
// gen: String with shapeless.labelled.KeyTag[Symbol with shapeless.tag.
//   Tagged[String("name")],String] :: Int with shapeless.labelled.
//   KeyTag[Symbol with shapeless.tag.Tagged[String("numCherries")],Int]
//   :: Boolean with shapeless.labelled.KeyTag[Symbol with shapeless.
//   tag.Tagged[String("inCone")],Boolean] :: shapeless.HNil = Sundae ::
//   1 :: false :: HNil
```

For clarity, the full type of the `HList` is:

```
// String  with KeyTag[Symbol with Tagged["name"], String]        ::
// Int     with KeyTag[Symbol with Tagged["numCherries"], Int] ::
// Boolean with KeyTag[Symbol with Tagged["inCone"], Boolean]  ::
// HNil
```

The type here is slightly more complex than we have seen. Instead of representing the field names with literal string types, shapeless is representing them with symbols tagged with literal string types. The details of the implementation aren't particularly important: we can still use Witness and FieldType to extract the tags, but they come out as Symbols instead of Strings[4].

5.3.1   Instances for *HLists*

Let's define JsonEncoder instances for HNil and ::. Our encoders are going to generate and manipulate JsonObjects, so we'll introduce a new type of encoder to make that easier:

```
trait JsonObjectEncoder[A] extends JsonEncoder[A] {
  def encode(value: A): JsonObject
}

def createObjectEncoder[A](fn: A => JsonObject): JsonObjectEncoder[A] =
  new JsonObjectEncoder[A] {
    def encode(value: A): JsonObject =
      fn(value)
  }
```

The definition for HNil is then straightforward:

```
import shapeless.{HList, ::, HNil, Lazy}

implicit val hnilEncoder: JsonObjectEncoder[HNil] =
  createObjectEncoder(hnil => JsonObject(Nil))
```

The definition of hlistEncoder involves a few moving parts so we'll go through it piece by piece. We'll start with the definition we might expect if we were using regular Generic:

---

[4]Future versions of shapeless may switch to using Strings as tags.

```
implicit def hlistObjectEncoder[H, T <: HList](
  implicit
  hEncoder: Lazy[JsonEncoder[H]],
  tEncoder: JsonObjectEncoder[T]
): JsonEncoder[H :: T] = ???
```

LabelledGeneric will give us an HList of tagged types, so let's start by introducing a new type variable for the key type:

```
import shapeless.Witness
import shapeless.labelled.FieldType

implicit def hlistObjectEncoder[K, H, T <: HList](
  implicit
  hEncoder: Lazy[JsonEncoder[H]],
  tEncoder: JsonObjectEncoder[T]
): JsonObjectEncoder[FieldType[K, H] :: T] = ???
```

In the body of our method we're going to need the value associated with K. We'll add an implicit Witness to do this for us:

```
implicit def hlistObjectEncoder[K, H, T <: HList](
  implicit
  witness: Witness.Aux[K],
  hEncoder: Lazy[JsonEncoder[H]],
  tEncoder: JsonObjectEncoder[T]
): JsonObjectEncoder[FieldType[K, H] :: T] = {
  val fieldName = witness.value
  ???
}
```

We can access the value of K using witness.value, but the compiler has no way of knowing what type of tag we're going to get. LabelledGeneric uses Symbols for tags, so we'll put a type bound on K and use symbol.name to convert it to a String:

```
implicit def hlistObjectEncoder[K <: Symbol, H, T <: HList](
  implicit
  witness: Witness.Aux[K],
```

```scala
  hEncoder: Lazy[JsonEncoder[H]],
  tEncoder: JsonObjectEncoder[T]
): JsonObjectEncoder[FieldType[K, H] :: T] = {
  val fieldName: String = witness.value.name
  ???
}
```

The rest of the definition uses the principles we covered in Chapter 3:

```scala
implicit def hlistObjectEncoder[K <: Symbol, H, T <: HList](
  implicit
  witness: Witness.Aux[K],
  hEncoder: Lazy[JsonEncoder[H]],
  tEncoder: JsonObjectEncoder[T]
): JsonObjectEncoder[FieldType[K, H] :: T] = {
  val fieldName: String = witness.value.name
  createObjectEncoder { hlist =>
    val head = hEncoder.value.encode(hlist.head)
    val tail = tEncoder.encode(hlist.tail)
    JsonObject((fieldName, head) :: tail.fields)
  }
}
```

5.3.2 Instances for concrete products

Finally let's turn to our generic instance. This is identical to the definitions we've seen before, except that we're using `LabelledGeneric` instead of `Generic`:

```scala
import shapeless.LabelledGeneric

implicit def genericObjectEncoder[A, H](
  implicit
  generic: LabelledGeneric.Aux[A, H],
  hEncoder: Lazy[JsonObjectEncoder[H]]
): JsonEncoder[A] =
  createObjectEncoder { value =>
    hEncoder.value.encode(generic.to(value))
  }
```

And that's all we need! With these definitions in place we can serialize instances of any case class and retain the field names in the resulting JSON:

```
JsonEncoder[IceCream].encode(iceCream)
// res14: JsonValue = JsonObject(List((name,JsonString(Sundae)), (
    numCherries,JsonNumber(1.0)), (inCone,JsonBoolean(false))))
```

5.4 Deriving coproduct instances with *LabelledGeneric*

Applying `LabelledGeneric` with `Coproducts` involves a mixture of the concepts we've covered already. Let's start by examining a `Coproduct` type derived by `LabelledGeneric`. We'll re-visit our Shape ADT from Chapter 3:

```
import shapeless.LabelledGeneric

sealed trait Shape
final case class Rectangle(width: Double, height: Double) extends Shape
final case class Circle(radius: Double) extends Shape

LabelledGeneric[Shape].to(Circle(1.0))
// res5: Rectangle with shapeless.labelled.KeyTag[Symbol with shapeless.
//     tag.Tagged[String("Rectangle")],Rectangle] :+: Circle with
//     shapeless.labelled.KeyTag[Symbol with shapeless.tag.Tagged[String("
//     Circle")],Circle] :+: shapeless.CNil = Inr(Inl(Circle(1.0)))
```

Here is that `Coproduct` type in a more readable format:

```
// Rectangle with KeyTag[Symbol with Tagged["Rectangle"], Rectangle] :+:
// Circle    with KeyTag[Symbol with Tagged["Circle"],    Circle]    :+:
// CNil
```

As you can see, the result is a `Coproduct` of the subtypes of Shape, each tagged with the type name. We can use this information to write `JsonEncoders` for `:+:` and `CNil`:

```scala
import shapeless.{Coproduct, :+:, CNil, Inl, Inr, Witness, Lazy}
import shapeless.labelled.FieldType

implicit val cnilObjectEncoder: JsonObjectEncoder[CNil] =
  createObjectEncoder(cnil => throw new Exception("Inconceivable!"))

implicit def coproductObjectEncoder[K <: Symbol, H, T <: Coproduct](
  implicit
  witness: Witness.Aux[K],
  hEncoder: Lazy[JsonEncoder[H]],
  tEncoder: JsonObjectEncoder[T]
): JsonObjectEncoder[FieldType[K, H] :+: T] = {
  val typeName = witness.value.name
  createObjectEncoder {
    case Inl(h) =>
      JsonObject(List(typeName -> hEncoder.value.encode(h)))

    case Inr(t) =>
      tEncoder.encode(t)
  }
}
```

coproductEncoder follows the same pattern as hlistEncoder. We have three type parameters: K for the type name, H for the value at the head of the HList, and T for the value at the tail. We use FieldType and :+: in the result type to declare the relationships between the three, and we use a Witness to access the runtime value of the type name. The result is an object containing a single key/value pair, the key being the type name and the value the result:

```scala
val shape: Shape = Circle(1.0)

JsonEncoder[Shape].encode(shape)
// res8: JsonValue = JsonObject(List((Circle,JsonObject(List((radius,
    JsonNumber(1.0)))))))
```

Other encodings are possible with a little more work. We can add a "type" field to the output, for example, or even allow the user to configure the format. Sam Halliday's spray-json-shapeless[5] is an excellent example of a codebase

---

[5]https://github.com/fommil/spray-json-shapeless

that is approachable while providing a great deal of flexibility.

5.5 Summary

In this chapter we discussed `LabelledGeneric`, a variant of `Generic` that exposes type and field names in its generic representations.

The names exposed by `LabelledGeneric` are encoded as type-level tags so we can target them during implicit resolution. We started the chapter discussing *literal types* and the way shapeless uses them in its tags. We also discussed the `Witness` type class, which is used to reify literal types as values.

Finally, we combined `LabelledGeneric`, literal types, and `Witness` to build a `JsonEcoder` library that includes sensible names in its output.

The key take home point from this chapter is that none of this code uses runtime reflection. Everything is implemented with types, implicits, and a small set of macros that are internal to shapeless. The code we're generating is consequently very fast and reliable at runtime.

Part II

Shapeless ops

Chapter 6

Working with *HLists* and *Coproducts*

In Part I we discussed methods for deriving type class instances for algebraic data types. We can use type class derivation to augment almost any type class, although in more complex cases we may have to write a lot of supporting code for manipulating HLists and Coproducts.

In Part II we'll look at the shapeless.ops package, which provides a set of helpful tools that we can use as building blocks. Each op comes in two parts: a *type class* that we can use during implicit resolution, and *extension methods* that we can call on HList and Coproduct.

There are three general sets of ops, available from three packages:

- shapeless.ops.hlist defines type classes for HLists. These can be used directly via extension methods on HList, defined in shapeless.syntax.hlist.

- shapeless.ops.coproduct defines type classes for Coproducts. These can be used directly via extension methods on Coproduct, defined in shapeless.syntax.coproduct.

- shapeless.ops.record defines type classes for shapeless records (HLists containing tagged elements—Section 5.2). These can be used

via extension methods on HList, imported from shapeless.record,
and defined in shapeless.syntax.record.

We don't have room in this book to cover all of the available ops. Fortunately,
in most cases the code is understandable and well documented. Rather than
provide an exhaustive guide, we will touch on the major theoretical and struc-
tural points and show you how to extract further information from the shapeless codebase.

6.1   Simple ops examples

HList has init and last extension methods based on two type
classes: shapeless.ops.hlist.Init and shapeless.ops.hlist.Last.
Coproduct has similar methods and type classes. These serve as perfect
examples of the ops pattern. Here are simplified definitions of the extension
methods:

```
package shapeless
package syntax

implicit class HListOps[L <: HList](l : L) {
  def last(implicit last: Last[L]): last.Out = last.apply(l)
  def init(implicit init: Init[L]): init.Out = init.apply(l)
}
```

The return type of each method is determined by a dependent type on the implicit parameter. The instances for each type class provide the actual mapping.
Here's the skeleton definition of Last as an example:

```
trait Last[L <: HList] {
  type Out
  def apply(in: L): Out
}

object Last {
  type Aux[L <: HList, O] = Last[L] { type Out = O }
  implicit def pair[H]: Aux[H :: HNil, H] = ???
```

```scala
implicit def list[H, T <: HList]
    (implicit last: Last[T]): Aux[H :: T, last.Out] = ???
}
```

We can make a couple of interesting observations about this implementation. First, we can typically implement ops type classes with a small number of instances (just two in this case). We can therefore package *all* of the required instances in the companion object of the type class, allowing us to call the corresponding extension methods without any imports from shapeless.ops:

```scala
import shapeless._

("Hello" :: 123 :: true :: HNil).last
// res0: Boolean = true

("Hello" :: 123 :: true :: HNil).init
// res1: String :: Int :: shapeless.HNil = Hello :: 123 :: HNil
```

Second, the type class is only defined for HLists with at least one element. This gives us a degree of static checking. If we try to call last on an empty HList, we get a compile error:

```scala
HNil.last
// <console>:16: error: Implicit not found: shapeless.Ops.Last[shapeless
//     .HNil.type]. shapeless.HNil.type is empty, so there is no last
//     element.
//          HNil.last
//               ^
```

6.2 Creating a custom op (the "lemma" pattern)

If we find a particular sequence of ops useful, we can package them up and re-provide them as another ops type class. This is an example of the "lemma" pattern, a term we introduced in Section 4.4.

Let's work through the creation of our own op as an exercise. We'll combine the power of Last and Init to create a Penultimate type class that retrieves the second-to-last element in an HList. Here's the type class definition, complete with Aux type alias and apply method:

```scala
import shapeless._

trait Penultimate[L] {
  type Out
  def apply(l: L): Out
}

object Penultimate {
  type Aux[L, O] = Penultimate[L] { type Out = O }

  def apply[L](implicit p: Penultimate[L]): Aux[L, p.Out] = p
}
```

Again, notice that the apply method has a return type of Aux[L, O] instead of Penultimate[L]. This ensures type members are visible on summoned instances as discussed in the callout in Section 4.2.

We only need to define one instance of Penultimate, combining Init and Last using the techniques covered in Section 4.3:

```scala
import shapeless.ops.hlist

implicit def hlistPenultimate[L <: HList, M <: HList, O](
  implicit
  init: hlist.Init.Aux[L, M],
  last: hlist.Last.Aux[M, O]
): Penultimate.Aux[L, O] =
  new Penultimate[L] {
    type Out = O
    def apply(l: L): O =
      last.apply(init.apply(l))
  }
```

We can use Penultimate as follows:

```
type BigList = String :: Int :: Boolean :: Double :: HNil

val bigList: BigList = "foo" :: 123 :: true :: 456.0 :: HNil

Penultimate[BigList].apply(bigList)
// res4: Boolean = true
```

Summoning an instance of `Penultimate` requires the compiler to summon instances for `Last` and `Init`, so we inherit the same level of type checking on short `HList`s:

```
type TinyList = String :: HNil

val tinyList = "bar" :: HNil

Penultimate[TinyList].apply(tinyList)
// <console>:21: error: could not find implicit value for parameter p:
//     Penultimate[TinyList]
//          Penultimate[TinyList].apply(tinyList)
//                    ^
```

We can make things more convenient for end users by defining an extension method on `HList`:

```
implicit class PenultimateOps[A](a: A) {
  def penultimate(implicit inst: Penultimate[A]): inst.Out =
    inst.apply(a)
}

bigList.penultimate
// res7: Boolean = true
```

We can also provide `Penultimate` for all product types by providing an instance based on `Generic`:

```
implicit def genericPenultimate[A, R, O](
  implicit
  generic: Generic.Aux[A, R],
  penultimate: Penultimate.Aux[R, O]
): Penultimate.Aux[A, O] =
```

```
  new Penultimate[A] {
    type Out = 0
    def apply(a: A): 0 =
      penultimate.apply(generic.to(a))
  }


case class IceCream(name: String, numCherries: Int, inCone: Boolean)

IceCream("Sundae", 1, false).penultimate
// res9: Int = 1
```

The important point here is that, by defining Penultimate as another type
class, we have created a reusable tool that we can apply elsewhere. Shapeless
provides many ops for many purposes, but it's easy to add our own to the
toolbox.

6.3 Case study: case class migrations

The power of ops type classes fully crystallizes when we chain them together
as building blocks for our own code. We'll finish this chapter with a compelling
example: a type class for performing "migrations" (aka "evolutions") on case
classes[1]. For example, if version 1 of our app contains the following case class:

```
case class IceCreamV1(name: String, numCherries: Int, inCone: Boolean)
```

our migration library should enable certain mechanical "upgrades" for free:

```
// Remove fields:
case class IceCreamV2a(name: String, inCone: Boolean)

// Reorder fields:
case class IceCreamV2b(name: String, inCone: Boolean, numCherries: Int)

// Insert fields (provided we can determine a default value):
case class IceCreamV2c(
```

---

[1]The term is stolen from "database migrations"—SQL scripts that automate upgrades to a
database schema.

```
name: String, inCone: Boolean, numCherries: Int, numWaffles: Int)
```

Ideally we'd like to be able to write code like this:

```
IceCreamV1("Sundae", 1, false).migrateTo[IceCreamV2a]
```

The type class should take care of the migration without additional boilerplate.

6.3.1   The type class

The Migration type class represents a transformation from a source to a des-
tination type. Both of these are going to be "input" types in our derivation, so
we model both as type parameters. We don't need an Aux type alias because
there are no type members to expose:

```
trait Migration[A, B] {
  def apply(a: A): B
}
```

We'll also introduce an extension method to make examples easier to read:

```
implicit class MigrationOps[A](a: A) {
  def migrateTo[B](implicit migration: Migration[A, B]): B =
    migration.apply(a)
}
```


6.3.2   Step 1. Removing fields

Let's build up the solution piece by piece, starting with field removal. We can
do this in several steps:

1. convert A to its generic representation;
2. filter the HList from step 1—only retain fields that are also in B;
3. convert the output of step 2 to B.

We can implement steps 1 and 3 with `Generic` or `LabelledGeneric`, and step 2 with an op called `Intersection`. `LabelledGeneric` seems a sensible choice because we need to identify fields by name:

```scala
import shapeless._
import shapeless.ops.hlist

implicit def genericMigration[A, B, ARepr <: HList, BRepr <: HList](
  implicit
  aGen  : LabelledGeneric.Aux[A, ARepr],
  bGen  : LabelledGeneric.Aux[B, BRepr],
  inter : hlist.Intersection.Aux[ARepr, BRepr, BRepr]
): Migration[A, B] = new Migration[A, B] {
  def apply(a: A): B =
    bGen.from(inter.apply(aGen.to(a)))
}
```

Take a moment to locate `Intersection`[2] in the shapeless codebase. Its Aux type alias takes three parameters: two input `HLists` and one output for the intersection type. In the example above we are specifying ARepr and BRepr as the input types and BRepr as the output type. This means implicit resolution will only succeed if B has an exact subset of the fields of A, specified with the exact same names in the same order:

```scala
IceCreamV1("Sundae", 1, true).migrateTo[IceCreamV2a]
// res6: IceCreamV2a = IceCreamV2a(Sundae,true)
```

We get a compile error if we try to use `Migration` with non-conforming types:

```scala
IceCreamV1("Sundae", 1, true).migrateTo[IceCreamV2b]
// <console>:23: error: could not find implicit value for parameter
//      migration: Migration[IceCreamV1,IceCreamV2b]
//          IceCreamV1("Sundae", 1, true).migrateTo[IceCreamV2b]
//                                        ^
```

---

[2]https://github.com/milessabin/shapeless/blob/shapeless-2.3.2/core/src/main/scala/shapeless/ops/hlists.scala#L1297-L1352

6.3.3 Step 2. Reordering fields

We need to lean on another ops type class to add support for reordering. The Align[3] op lets us reorder the fields in one HList to match the order they appear in another HList. We can redefine our instance using Align as follows:

```scala
implicit def genericMigration[
  A, B,
  ARepr <: HList, BRepr <: HList,
  Unaligned <: HList
](
  implicit
  aGen    : LabelledGeneric.Aux[A, ARepr],
  bGen    : LabelledGeneric.Aux[B, BRepr],
  inter   : hlist.Intersection.Aux[ARepr, BRepr, Unaligned],
  align   : hlist.Align[Unaligned, BRepr]
): Migration[A, B] = new Migration[A, B] {
  def apply(a: A): B =
    bGen.from(align.apply(inter.apply(aGen.to(a))))
}
```

We introduce a new type parameter called Unaligned to represent the intersection of ARepr and BRepr before alignment, and use Align to convert Unaligned to BRepr. With this modified definition of Migration we can both remove and reorder fields:

```scala
IceCreamV1("Sundae", 1, true).migrateTo[IceCreamV2a]
// res8: IceCreamV2a = IceCreamV2a(Sundae,true)

IceCreamV1("Sundae", 1, true).migrateTo[IceCreamV2b]
// res9: IceCreamV2b = IceCreamV2b(Sundae,true,1)
```

However, if we try to add fields we still get a failure:

```scala
IceCreamV1("Sundae", 1, true).migrateTo[IceCreamV2c]
// <console>:25: error: could not find implicit value for parameter
//     migration: Migration[IceCreamV1,IceCreamV2c]
```

---

[3]https://github.com/milessabin/shapeless/blob/shapeless-2.3.2/core/src/main/scala/shapeless/ops/hlists.scala#L1973-L1997

```
//         IceCreamV1("Sundae", 1, true).migrateTo[IceCreamV2c]
//                                       ^
```

6.3.4   Step 3. Adding new fields

We need a mechanism for calculating default values to support the addition
of new fields. Shapeless doesn't provide a type class for this, but Cats does in
the form of a `Monoid`. Here's a simplified definition:

```scala
package cats

trait Monoid[A] {
  def empty: A
  def combine(x: A, y: A): A
}
```

`Monoid` defines two operations: `empty` for creating a "zero" value and `combine`
for "adding" two values. We only need `empty` in our code, but it will be trivial
to define `combine` as well.

Cats provides instances of `Monoid` for all the primitive types we care about
(`Int`, `Double`, `Boolean`, and `String`). We can define instances for `HNil` and
`::` using the techniques from Chapter 5:

```scala
import cats.Monoid
import cats.instances.all._
import shapeless.labelled.{field, FieldType}

def createMonoid[A](zero: A)(add: (A, A) => A): Monoid[A] =
  new Monoid[A] {
    def empty = zero
    def combine(x: A, y: A): A = add(x, y)
  }

implicit val hnilMonoid: Monoid[HNil] =
  createMonoid[HNil](HNil)((x, y) => HNil)

implicit def emptyHList[K <: Symbol, H, T <: HList](
  implicit
```

```
  hMonoid: Lazy[Monoid[H]],
  tMonoid: Monoid[T]
): Monoid[FieldType[K, H] :: T] =
  createMonoid(field[K](hMonoid.value.empty) :: tMonoid.empty) {
    (x, y) =>
      field[K](hMonoid.value.combine(x.head, y.head)) ::
        tMonoid.combine(x.tail, y.tail)
  }
```

We need to combine Monoid[4] with a couple of other ops to complete our final implementation of Migration. Here's the full list of steps:

1. use LabelledGeneric to convert A to its generic representation;
2. use Intersection to calculate an HList of fields common to A and B;
3. calculate the types of fields that appear in B but not in A;
4. use Monoid to calculate a default value of the type from step 3;
5. append the common fields from step 2 to the new field from step 4;
6. use Align to reorder the fields from step 5 in the same order as B;
7. use LabelledGeneric to convert the output of step 6 to B.

We've already seen how to implement steps 1, 2, 4, 6, and 7. We can implement step 3 using an op called Diff that is very similar to Intersection, and step 5 using another op called Prepend. Here's the complete solution:

```
implicit def genericMigration[
  A, B, ARepr <: HList, BRepr <: HList,
  Common <: HList, Added <: HList, Unaligned <: HList
](
  implicit
  aGen    : LabelledGeneric.Aux[A, ARepr],
  bGen    : LabelledGeneric.Aux[B, BRepr],
  inter   : hlist.Intersection.Aux[ARepr, BRepr, Common],
  diff    : hlist.Diff.Aux[BRepr, Common, Added],
  monoid  : Monoid[Added],
  prepend : hlist.Prepend.Aux[Added, Common, Unaligned],
  align   : hlist.Align[Unaligned, BRepr]
): Migration[A, B] =
```

---

[4]Pun intended.

```
  new Migration[A, B] {
    def apply(a: A): B =
      bGen.from(align(prepend(monoid.empty, inter(aGen.to(a)))))
  }
```

Note that this code doesn't use every type class at the value level. We use `Diff` to calculate the Added data type, but we don't actually need `diff.apply` at run time. Instead we use our `Monoid` to summon an instance of `Added`.

With this final version of the type class instance in place we can use `Migration` for all the use cases we set out at the beginning of the case study:

```
IceCreamV1("Sundae", 1, true).migrateTo[IceCreamV2a]
// res14: IceCreamV2a = IceCreamV2a(Sundae,true)

IceCreamV1("Sundae", 1, true).migrateTo[IceCreamV2b]
// res15: IceCreamV2b = IceCreamV2b(Sundae,true,1)

IceCreamV1("Sundae", 1, true).migrateTo[IceCreamV2c]
// res16: IceCreamV2c = IceCreamV2c(Sundae,true,1,0)
```

It's amazing what we can create with ops type classes. `Migration` has a single `implicit def` with a single line of value-level implementation. It allows us to automate migrations between *any* pair of case classes, in roughly the same amount of code we'd write to handle a *single* pair of types using the standard library. Such is the power of shapeless!

6.4   Record ops

We've spent some time in this chapter looking at type classes from the `shapeless.ops.hlist` and `shapeless.ops.coproduct` packages. We mustn't leave without mentioning a third important package: `shapeless.ops.record`.

Shapeless' "record ops" provide Map-like operations on `HLists` of tagged elements. Here are a handful of examples involving ice creams:

```
import shapeless._

case class IceCream(name: String, numCherries: Int, inCone: Boolean)

val sundae = LabelledGeneric[IceCream].
  to(IceCream("Sundae", 1, false))
// sundae: String with shapeless.labelled.KeyTag[Symbol with shapeless.
//     tag.Tagged[String("name")],String] :: Int with shapeless.labelled.
//     KeyTag[Symbol with shapeless.tag.Tagged[String("numCherries")],Int]
//     :: Boolean with shapeless.labelled.KeyTag[Symbol with shapeless.
//     tag.Tagged[String("inCone")],Boolean] :: shapeless.HNil = Sundae ::
//     1 :: false :: HNil
```

Unlike the `HList` and `Coproduct` ops we have seen already, record ops syntax requires an explicit import from `shapeless.record`:

```
import shapeless.record._
```

6.4.1 Selecting fields

The `get` extension method and its corresponding `Selector` type class allow us to fetch a field by tag:

```
sundae.get('name)
// res1: String = Sundae

sundae.get('numCherries)
// res2: Int = 1
```

Attempting to access an undefined field causes a compile error as we might expect:

```
sundae.get('nomCherries)
// <console>:20: error: No field Symbol with shapeless.tag.Tagged[String
//     ("nomCherries")] in record String with shapeless.labelled.KeyTag[
//     Symbol with shapeless.tag.Tagged[String("name")],String] :: Int
//     with shapeless.labelled.KeyTag[Symbol with shapeless.tag.Tagged[
//     String("numCherries")],Int] :: Boolean with shapeless.labelled.
```

```
    KeyTag[Symbol with shapeless.tag.Tagged[String("inCone")],Boolean]
    :: shapeless.HNil
//      sundae.get('nomCherries)
//                ^
```

6.4.2 Updating and removing fields

The updated method and Updater type class allow us to modify fields by key.
The remove method and Remover type class allow us to delete fields by key:

```
sundae.updated('numCherries, 3)
// res4: String with shapeless.labelled.KeyTag[Symbol with shapeless.tag
//     .Tagged[String("name")],String] :: Int with shapeless.labelled.
//     KeyTag[Symbol with shapeless.tag.Tagged[String("numCherries")],Int]
//     :: Boolean with shapeless.labelled.KeyTag[Symbol with shapeless.
//     tag.Tagged[String("inCone")],Boolean] :: shapeless.HNil = Sundae ::
//     3 :: false :: HNil

sundae.remove('inCone)
// res5: (Boolean, String with shapeless.labelled.KeyTag[Symbol with
//     shapeless.tag.Tagged[String("name")],String] :: Int with shapeless.
//     labelled.KeyTag[Symbol with shapeless.tag.Tagged[String("
//     numCherries")],Int] :: shapeless.HNil) = (false,Sundae :: 1 :: HNil
//     )
```

The updateWith method and Modifier type class allow us to modify a field
with an update function:

```
sundae.updateWith('name)("MASSIVE " + _)
// res6: String with shapeless.labelled.KeyTag[Symbol with shapeless.tag
//     .Tagged[String("name")],String] :: Int with shapeless.labelled.
//     KeyTag[Symbol with shapeless.tag.Tagged[String("numCherries")],Int]
//     :: Boolean with shapeless.labelled.KeyTag[Symbol with shapeless.
//     tag.Tagged[String("inCone")],Boolean] :: shapeless.HNil = MASSIVE
//     Sundae :: 1 :: false :: HNil
```

6.4.3 Converting to a regular *Map*

The toMap method and ToMap type class allow us to convert a record to a Map:

```
sundae.toMap
// res7: Map[Symbol with shapeless.tag.Tagged[_ >: String("inCone") with
      String("numCherries") with String("name") <: String],Any] = Map('
      inCone -> false, 'numCherries -> 1, 'name -> Sundae)
```

6.4.4 Other operations

There are other record ops that we don't have room to cover here. We can rename fields, merge records, map over their values, and much more. See the source code of `shapeless.ops.record` and `shapeless.syntax.record` for more information.

6.5 Summary

In this chapter we explored a few of the type classes that are provided in the `shapeless.ops` package. We looked at `Last` and `Init` as two simple examples of the ops pattern, and built our own `Penultimate` and `Migration` type classes by chaining together existing building blocks.

Many of the ops type classes share a similar pattern to the ops we've seen here. The easiest way to learn them is to look at the source code in `shapeless.ops` and `shapeless.syntax`.

In the next chapters we will look at two suites of ops type classes that require further theoretical discussion. Chapter 7 discusses functional operations such as `map` and `flatMap` on `HLists`, and Chapter 8 discusses how to implement type classes that require type level representations of numbers. This knowledge will help us gain a more complete understanding of the variety of type classes from `shapeless.ops`.

Chapter 7

Functional operations on *HLists*

"Regular" Scala programs make heavy use of functional operations like map and flatMap. A question arises: can we perform similar operations on HLists? The answer is "yes", although we have to do things a little differently than in regular Scala. Unsurprisingly the mechanisms we use are type class based and there are a suite of ops type classes to help us out.

Before we delve in to the type classes themselves, we need to discuss how shapeless represents *polymorphic functions* suitable for mapping over heterogeneous data structures.

7.1 Motivation: mapping over an *HList*

We'll motivate the discussion of polymorphic functions by looking at the map method. Figure 7.1 shows a type chart for mapping over a regular list. We start with a List[A], supply a function A => B, and end up with a List[B].

The heterogeneous element types in an HList cause this model to break down. Scala functions have fixed input and output types, so the result of our map will have to have the same element type in every position.

Ideally we'd like a map operation like the one shown in Figure 7.2, where the function inspects the type of each input and uses it to determine the type of

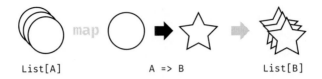

Figure 7.1: Mapping over a regular list ("monomorphic" map)

each output. This gives us a closed, composable transformation that retains the heterogeneous nature of the HList.

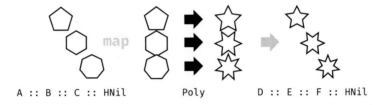

Figure 7.2: Mapping over a heterogeneous list ("polymorphic" map)

Unfortunately we can't use Scala functions to implement this kind of operation. We need some new infrastructure.

7.2 Polymorphic functions

Shapeless provides a type called Poly for representing *polymorphic functions*, where the result type depends on the parameter types. Here is a simplified explanation of how it works. Note that the next section doesn't contain real shapeless code—we're eliding much of the flexibility and ease of use that comes with real shapeless Polys to create a simplified API for illustrative purposes.

7.2.1 How *Poly* works

At its core, a Poly is an object with a generic apply method. In addition to its regular parameter of type A, Poly accepts an implicit parameter of type

Case[A]:

```
// This is not real shapeless code.
// It's just for demonstration.

trait Case[P, A] {
  type Result
  def apply(a: A): Result
}

trait Poly {
  def apply[A](arg: A)(implicit cse: Case[this.type, A]): cse.Result =
    cse.apply(arg)
}
```

When we define an actual Poly, we provide instances of Case for each parameter type we care about. These implement the actual function body:

```
// This is not real shapeless code.
// It's just for demonstration.

object myPoly extends Poly {
  implicit def intCase =
    new Case[this.type, Int] {
      type Result = Double
      def apply(num: Int): Double = num / 2.0
    }

  implicit def stringCase =
    new Case[this.type, String] {
      type Result = Int
      def apply(str: String): Int = str.length
    }
}
```

When we call myPoly.apply, the compiler searches for the relevant implicit Case and inserts it as usual:

```
myPoly.apply(123)
// res8: Double = 61.5
```

There is some subtle scoping behaviour here that allows the compiler to locate instances of Case without any additional imports. Case has an extra type
parameter P referencing the singleton type of the Poly. The implicit scope
for Case[P, A] includes the companion objects for Case, P, and A. We've as-
signed P to be myPoly.type and the companion object for myPoly.type is
myPoly itself. In other words, Cases defined in the body of the Poly are always in scope no matter where the call site is.

7.2.2 *Poly* syntax

The code above isn't real shapeless code. Fortunately, shapeless makes Polys
much simpler to define. Here's our myPoly function rewritten in proper syntax:

```
import shapeless._

object myPoly extends Poly1 {
  implicit val intCase: Case.Aux[Int, Double] =
    at(num => num / 2.0)

  implicit val stringCase: Case.Aux[String, Int] =
    at(str => str.length)
}
```

There are a few key differences with our earlier toy syntax:

1. We're extending a trait called Poly1 instead of Poly. Shapeless has a
   Poly type and a set of subtypes, Poly1 through Poly22, supporting
   different arities of polymorphic function.

2. The Case.Aux types doesn't seem to reference the singleton type of
   the Poly. Case.Aux is actually a type alias defined within the body of
   Poly1. The singleton type is there—we just don't see it.

3. We're using a helper method, at, to define cases. This acts as an instance constructor method as discussed in Section 3.1.2), which elimi-
   nates a lot of boilerplate.

Syntactic differences aside, the shapeless version of myPoly is functionally identical to our toy version. We can call it with an Int or String parameter and get back a result of the corresponding return type:

```
myPoly.apply(123)
// res10: myPoly.intCase.Result = 61.5

myPoly.apply("hello")
// res11: myPoly.stringCase.Result = 5
```

Shapeless also supports Polys with more than one parameter. Here is a binary example:

```
object multiply extends Poly2 {
  implicit val intIntCase: Case.Aux[Int, Int, Int] =
    at((a, b) => a * b)

  implicit val intStrCase: Case.Aux[Int, String, String] =
    at((a, b) => b.toString * a)
}

multiply(3, 4)
// res12: multiply.intIntCase.Result = 12

multiply(3, "4")
// res13: multiply.intStrCase.Result = 444
```

Because Cases are just implicit values, we can define cases based on type classes and do all of the advanced implicit resolution covered in previous chapters. Here's a simple example that totals numbers in different contexts:

```
import scala.math.Numeric

object total extends Poly1 {
  implicit def base[A](implicit num: Numeric[A]):
      Case.Aux[A, Double] =
    at(num.toDouble)

  implicit def option[A](implicit num: Numeric[A]):
      Case.Aux[Option[A], Double] =
```

```scala
    at(opt => opt.map(num.toDouble).getOrElse(0.0))

  implicit def list[A](implicit num: Numeric[A]):
      Case.Aux[List[A], Double] =
      at(list => num.toDouble(list.sum))
}

total(10)
// res15: Double = 10.0

total(Option(20.0))
// res16: Double = 20.0

total(List(1L, 2L, 3L))
// res17: Double = 6.0
```

Idiosyncrasies of type inference

Poly pushes Scala's type inference out of its comfort zone. We can easily confuse the compiler by asking it to do too much inference at once. For example, the following code compiles ok:

```scala
val a = myPoly.apply(123)
val b: Double = a
```

However, combining the two lines causes a compilation error:

```scala
val a: Double = myPoly.apply(123)
// <console>:17: error: type mismatch;
//  found   : Int(123)
//  required: myPoly.ProductCase.Aux[shapeless.HNil,?]
//     (which expands to)  shapeless.poly.Case[myPoly.type,
     shapeless.HNil]{type Result = ?}
//         val a: Double = myPoly.apply(123)
//                                       ^
```

If we add a type annotation, the code compiles again:

```
val a: Double = myPoly.apply[Int](123)
// a: Double = 61.5
```

This behaviour is confusing and annoying. Unfortunately there are no concrete rules to follow to avoid problems. The only general guideline is to try not to over-constrain the compiler, solve one constraint at a time, and give it a hint when it gets stuck.

7.3 Mapping and flatMapping using *Poly*

Shapeless provides a suite of functional operations based on `Poly`, each implemented as an ops type class. Let's look at `map` and `flatMap` as examples. Here's `map`:

```
import shapeless._

object sizeOf extends Poly1 {
  implicit val intCase: Case.Aux[Int, Int] =
    at(identity)

  implicit val stringCase: Case.Aux[String, Int] =
    at(_.length)

  implicit val booleanCase: Case.Aux[Boolean, Int] =
    at(bool => if(bool) 1 else 0)
}

(10 :: "hello" :: true :: HNil).map(sizeOf)
// res1: Int :: Int :: Int :: shapeless.HNil = 10 :: 5 :: 1 :: HNil
```

Note that the elements in the resulting `HList` have types matching the `Cases` in `sizeOf`. We can use `map` with any `Poly` that provides `Cases` for every member of our starting `HList`. If the compiler can't find a `Case` for a particular member, we get a compile error:

```
(1.5 :: HNil).map(sizeOf)
// <console>:17: error: could not find implicit value for parameter
      mapper: shapeless.ops.hlist.Mapper[sizeOf.type,Double :: shapeless.
      HNil]
//         (1.5 :: HNil).map(sizeOf)
//                      ^
```

We can also `flatMap` over an `HList`, as long as every corresponding case in our `Poly` returns another `HList`:

```
object valueAndSizeOf extends Poly1 {
  implicit val intCase: Case.Aux[Int, Int :: Int :: HNil] =
    at(num => num :: num :: HNil)

  implicit val stringCase: Case.Aux[String, String :: Int :: HNil] =
    at(str => str :: str.length :: HNil)

  implicit val booleanCase: Case.Aux[Boolean, Boolean :: Int :: HNil] =
    at(bool => bool :: (if(bool) 1 else 0) :: HNil)
}

(10 :: "hello" :: true :: HNil).flatMap(valueAndSizeOf)
// res3: Int :: Int :: String :: Int :: Boolean :: Int :: shapeless.HNil
        = 10 :: 10 :: hello :: 5 :: true :: 1 :: HNil
```

Again, we get a compilation error if there is a missing case or one of the cases doesn't return an `HList`:

```
// Using the wrong Poly with flatMap:
(10 :: "hello" :: true :: HNil).flatMap(sizeOf)
// <console>:18: error: could not find implicit value for parameter
      mapper: shapeless.ops.hlist.FlatMapper[sizeOf.type,Int :: String ::
      Boolean :: shapeless.HNil]
//         (10 :: "hello" :: true :: HNil).flatMap(sizeOf)
//                                         ^
```

`map` and `flatMap` are based on type classes called `Mapper` and `FlatMapper` respectively. We'll see an example that makes direct use of `Mapper` in Section 7.5.

7.4 Folding using *Poly*

In addition to map and flatMap, shapeless also provides foldLeft and foldRight operations based on Poly2:

```
import shapeless._

object sum extends Poly2 {
  implicit val intIntCase: Case.Aux[Int, Int, Int] =
    at((a, b) => a + b)

  implicit val intStringCase: Case.Aux[Int, String, Int] =
    at((a, b) => a + b.length)
}

(10 :: "hello" :: 100 :: HNil).foldLeft(0)(sum)
// res7: Int = 115
```

We can also reduceLeft, reduceRight, foldMap, and so on. Each operation has its own associated type class. We'll leave it as an exercise to the reader to investigate the available operations.

7.5 Defining type classes using *Poly*

We can use Poly and type classes like Mapper and FlatMapper as building blocks for our own type classes. As an example let's build a type class for mapping from one case class to another:

```
trait ProductMapper[A, B, P] {
  def apply(a: A): B
}
```

We can create an instance of ProductMapper using Mapper and a pair of Generics:

```scala
import shapeless._
import shapeless.ops.hlist

implicit def genericProductMapper[
  A, B,
  P <: Poly,
  ARepr <: HList,
  BRepr <: HList
](
  implicit
  aGen: Generic.Aux[A, ARepr],
  bGen: Generic.Aux[B, BRepr],
  mapper: hlist.Mapper.Aux[P, ARepr, BRepr]
): ProductMapper[A, B, P] =
  new ProductMapper[A, B, P] {
    def apply(a: A): B =
      bGen.from(mapper.apply(aGen.to(a)))
  }
```

Interestingly, although we define a type P for our Poly, we don't reference any values of type P anywhere in our code. The Mapper type class uses implicit resolution to find Cases, so the compiler only needs to know the singleton type of P to locate the relevant instances.

Let's create an extension method to make ProductMapper easier to use. We only want the user to specify the type of B at the call site, so we use some indirection to allow the compiler to infer the type of the Poly from a value parameter:

```scala
implicit class ProductMapperOps[A](a: A) {
  class Builder[B] {
    def apply[P <: Poly](poly: P)
        (implicit pm: ProductMapper[A, B, P]): B =
      pm.apply(a)
  }

  def mapTo[B]: Builder[B] = new Builder[B]
}
```

Here's an example of the method's use:

```
object conversions extends Poly1 {
  implicit val intCase:  Case.Aux[Int, Boolean]    = at(_ > 0)
  implicit val boolCase: Case.Aux[Boolean, Int]    = at(if(_) 1 else 0)
  implicit val strCase:  Case.Aux[String, String] = at(identity)
}


case class IceCream1(name: String, numCherries: Int, inCone: Boolean)
case class IceCream2(name: String, hasCherries: Boolean, numCones: Int)


IceCream1("Sundae", 1, false).mapTo[IceCream2](conversions)
// res2: IceCream2 = IceCream2(Sundae,true,0)
```

The mapTo syntax looks like a single method call, but is actually two calls: one
call to mapTo to fix the B type parameter, and one call to Builder.apply to
specify the Poly. Some of shapeless' built-in ops extension methods use similar tricks to provide the user with convenient syntax.

7.6 Summary

In this chapter we discussed *polymorphic functions* whose return types vary
based on the types of their parameters. We saw how shapeless' Poly type is
defined, and how it is used to implement functional operations such as map,
flatMap, foldLeft, and foldRight.

Each operation is implemented as an extension method on HList, based on
a corresponding type class: Mapper, FlatMapper, LeftFolder, and so on.
We can use these type classes, Poly, and the techniques from Section 4.3
to create our own type classes involving sequences of sophisticated transfor-
mations.

Chapter 8

Counting with types

From time to time we need to count things at the type level. For example, we may need to know the length of an HList or the number of terms we have expanded so far in a computation. We can represent numbers as values easily enough, but if we want to influence implicit resolution we need to represent them at the type level. This chapter covers the theory behind counting with types, and provides some compelling use cases for type class derivation.

8.1   Representing numbers as types

Shapeless uses "Church encoding" to represent natural numbers at the type level. It provides a type Nat with two subtypes: _0 representing zero, and Succ[N] representing N+1:

```
import shapeless.{Nat, Succ}

type Zero = Nat._0
type One  = Succ[Zero]
type Two  = Succ[One]
// etc...
```

Shapeless provides aliases for the first 22 Nats as Nat._N:

```
Nat._1
Nat._2
Nat._3
// etc...
```

Nat has no runtime semantics. We have to use the ToInt type class to convert a Nat to a runtime Int:

```
import shapeless.ops.nat.ToInt

val toInt = ToInt[Two]

toInt.apply()
// res7: Int = 2
```

The Nat.toInt method provides a convenient shorthand for calling toInt.apply(). It accepts the instance of ToInt as an implicit parameter:

```
Nat.toInt[Nat._3]
// res8: Int = 3
```

8.2   Length of generic representations

One use case for Nat is determining the lengths of HLists and Coproducts. Shapeless provides the shapeless.ops.hlist.Length and shapeless.ops.copro type classes for this:

```
import shapeless._
import shapeless.ops.{hlist, coproduct, nat}

val hlistLength = hlist.Length[String :: Int :: Boolean :: HNil]
// hlistLength: shapeless.ops.hlist.Length[String :: Int :: Boolean ::
//     shapeless.HNil]{type Out = shapeless.Succ[shapeless.Succ[shapeless.
//     Succ[shapeless._0]]]} = shapeless.ops.hlist$Length$$anon$3@23180351

val coproductLength = coproduct.Length[Double :+: Char :+: CNil]
// coproductLength: shapeless.ops.coproduct.Length[Double :+: Char :+:
//     shapeless.CNil]{type Out = shapeless.Succ[shapeless.Succ[shapeless.
```

```
  _0]]} = shapeless.ops.coproduct$Length$$anon$29@6b89f407
```

Instances of Length have a type member Out that represents the length as a Nat:

```
Nat.toInt[hlistLength.Out]
// res0: Int = 3

Nat.toInt[coproductLength.Out]
// res1: Int = 2
```

Let's use this in a concrete example. We'll create a SizeOf type class that counts the number of fields in a case class and exposes it as a simple Int:

```
trait SizeOf[A] {
  def value: Int
}

def sizeOf[A](implicit size: SizeOf[A]): Int = size.value
```

To create an instance of SizeOf we need three things:

1. a Generic to calculate the corresponding HList type;
2. a Length to calculate the length of the HList as a Nat;
3. a ToInt to convert the Nat to an Int.

Here's a working implementation written in the style described in Chapter 4:

```
implicit def genericSizeOf[A, L <: HList, N <: Nat](
  implicit
  generic: Generic.Aux[A, L],
  size: hlist.Length.Aux[L, N],
  sizeToInt: nat.ToInt[N]
): SizeOf[A] =
  new SizeOf[A] {
    val value = sizeToInt.apply()
  }
```

We can test our code as follows:

```scala
case class IceCream(name: String, numCherries: Int, inCone: Boolean)

sizeOf[IceCream]
// res3: Int = 3
```

8.3   Case study: random value generator

Property-based testing libraries like ScalaCheck[1] use type classes to generate random data for unit tests. For example, ScalaCheck provides the Arbitrary type class that we can use as follows:

```scala
import org.scalacheck._

for(i <- 1 to 3) println(Arbitrary.arbitrary[Int].sample)
// Some(1)
// Some(1813066787)
// Some(1637191929)

for(i <- 1 to 3) println(Arbitrary.arbitrary[(Boolean, Byte)].sample)
// Some((true,127))
// Some((false,83))
// Some((false,-128))
```

ScalaCheck provides built-in instances of Arbitrary for a wide range of standard Scala types. However, creating instances of Arbitrary for user ADTs is still a time-consuming manual process. This makes shapeless integration via libraries like scalacheck-shapeless[2] very attractive.

In this section we will create a simple Random type class to generate random values of user-defined ADTs. We will show how Length and Nat form a crucial part of the implementation. As usual we start with the definition of the type class itself:

---

[1]https://scalacheck.org
[2]https://github.com/alexarchambault/scalacheck-shapeless

```scala
trait Random[A] {
  def get: A
}

def random[A](implicit r: Random[A]): A = r.get
```

8.3.1 Simple random values

Let's start with some basic instances of Random:

```scala
// Instance constructor:
def createRandom[A](func: () => A): Random[A] =
  new Random[A] {
    def get = func()
  }

// Random numbers from 0 to 9:
implicit val intRandom: Random[Int] =
  createRandom(() => scala.util.Random.nextInt(10))

// Random characters from A to Z:
implicit val charRandom: Random[Char] =
  createRandom(() => ('A'.toInt + scala.util.Random.nextInt(26)).toChar)

// Random booleans:
implicit val booleanRandom: Random[Boolean] =
  createRandom(() => scala.util.Random.nextBoolean)
```

We can use these simple generators via the random method as follows:

```scala
for(i <- 1 to 3) println(random[Int])
// 0
// 8
// 9

for(i <- 1 to 3) println(random[Char])
// V
// N
// J
```

8.3.2   Random products

We can create random values for products using the `Generic` and `HList` techniques from Chapter 3:

```scala
import shapeless._

implicit def genericRandom[A, R](
  implicit
  gen: Generic.Aux[A, R],
  random: Lazy[Random[R]]
): Random[A] =
  createRandom(() => gen.from(random.value.get))

implicit val hnilRandom: Random[HNil] =
  createRandom(() => HNil)

implicit def hlistRandom[H, T <: HList](
  implicit
  hRandom: Lazy[Random[H]],
  tRandom: Random[T]
): Random[H :: T] =
  createRandom(() => hRandom.value.get :: tRandom.get)
```

This gets us as far as summoning random instances for case classes:

```scala
case class Cell(col: Char, row: Int)

for(i <- 1 to 5) println(random[Cell])
// Cell(H,1)
// Cell(D,4)
// Cell(D,7)
// Cell(V,2)
// Cell(R,4)
```

8.3.3   Random coproducts

This is where we start hitting problems. Generating a random instance of a coproduct involves choosing a random subtype. Let's start with a naïve implementation:

```scala
implicit val cnilRandom: Random[CNil] =
  createRandom(() => throw new Exception("Inconceivable!"))

implicit def coproductRandom[H, T <: Coproduct](
  implicit
  hRandom: Lazy[Random[H]],
  tRandom: Random[T]
): Random[H :+: T] =
  createRandom { () =>
    val chooseH = scala.util.Random.nextDouble < 0.5
    if(chooseH) Inl(hRandom.value.get) else Inr(tRandom.get)
  }
```

There problems with this implementation lie in the 50/50 choice in calculating chooseH. This creates an uneven probability distribution. For example, consider the following type:

```scala
sealed trait Light
case object Red extends Light
case object Amber extends Light
case object Green extends Light
```

The Repr for Light is Red :+: Amber :+: Green :+: CNil. An instance of Random for this type will choose Red 50% of the time and Amber :+: Green :+: CNil 50% of the time. A correct distribution would be 33% Red and 67% Amber :+: Green :+: CNil.

And that's not all. If we look at the overall probability distribution we see something even more alarming:

- Red is chosen 1/2 of the time
- Amber is chosen 1/4 of the time
- Green is chosen 1/8 of the time
- *CNil is chosen 1/16 of the time*

Our coproduct instances will throw exceptions 6.75% of the time!

```
for(i <- 1 to 100) random[Light]
// java.lang.Exception: Inconceivable!
//    ...
```

To fix this problem we have to alter the probability of choosing H over T. The correct behaviour should be to choose H 1/n of the time, where n is the length of the coproduct. This ensures an even probability distribution across the subtypes of the coproduct. It also ensures we choose the head of a single-subtype Coproduct 100% of the time, which means we never call cnilProduct.get. Here's an updated implementation:

```
import shapeless.ops.coproduct
import shapeless.ops.nat.ToInt

implicit def coproductRandom[H, T <: Coproduct, L <: Nat](
  implicit
  hRandom: Lazy[Random[H]],
  tRandom: Random[T],
  tLength: coproduct.Length.Aux[T, L],
  tLengthAsInt: ToInt[L]
): Random[H :+: T] = {
  createRandom { () =>
    val length = 1 + tLengthAsInt()
    val chooseH = scala.util.Random.nextDouble < (1.0 / length)
    if(chooseH) Inl(hRandom.value.get) else Inr(tRandom.get)
  }
}
```

With these modifications we can generate random values of any product or coproduct:

```
for(i <- 1 to 5) println(random[Light])
// Green
// Red
// Red
// Red
// Green
```

Generating test data for ScalaCheck normally requires a great deal of boilerplate. Random value generation is a compelling use case for shapeless of which Nat forms an essential component.

8.4 Other operations involving *Nat*

Shapeless provides a suite of other operations based on Nat. The apply methods on HList and Coproduct can accept Nats as value or type parameters:

```
import shapeless._

val hlist = 123 :: "foo" :: true :: 'x' :: HNil

hlist.apply[Nat._1]
// res1: String = foo

hlist.apply(Nat._3)
// res2: Char = x
```

There are also operations such as take, drop, slice, and updatedAt:

```
hlist.take(Nat._3).drop(Nat._1)
// res3: String :: Boolean :: shapeless.HNil = foo :: true :: HNil

hlist.updatedAt(Nat._1, "bar").updatedAt(Nat._2, "baz")
// res4: Int :: String :: String :: Char :: shapeless.HNil = 123 :: bar
//    :: baz :: x :: HNil
```

These operations and their associated type classes are useful for manipulating individual elements within a product or coproduct.

8.5 Summary

In this chapter we discussed how shapeless represents natural numbers and how we can use them in type classes. We saw some predefined ops type classes that let us do things like calculate lengths and access elements by index, and created our own type classes that use Nat in other ways.

Between Nat, Poly, and the variety of types we have seen in the last few chapters, we have seen just a small fraction of the toolbox provided in shapeless.ops. There are many other ops type classes that provide a comprehensive foundation on which to build our own code. However, the theory laid out here is enough to understand the majority of ops needed to derive our own type classes. The source code in the shapeless.ops packages should now be approachable enough to pick up other useful ops.

Prepare for launch!

With Part II's look at shapeless.ops we have arrived at the end of this guide. We hope you found it useful for understanding this fascinating and powerful library, and wish you all the best on your future journeys as a type astronaut.

As functional programmers we value abstraction above all else. Concepts like functors and monads arise from years of programming research: writing code, spotting patterns, and making abstractions to remove redundancy. Shapeless raises the bar for abstraction in Scala. Tools like Generic and LabelledGeneric provide an interface for abstracting over data types that were previously frustratingly unique and distinct.

There have traditionally been two barriers to entry for aspiring new shapeless users. The first is the wealth of theoretical knowledge and implementation detail required to understand the patterns we need. Hopefully this guide has helped in this regard.

The second barrier is the fear and uncertainty surrounding a library that is seen as "academic" or "advanced". We can overcome this by sharing knowledge—use cases, pros and cons, implementation strategies, and so on—to widen the understanding of this valuable tool. So please share this book with a friend... and let's scrap some boilerplate together!